M000248920

PATHWAYS

SECOND EDITION

Listening, Speaking, and Critical Thinking

BECKY TARVER CHASE

NATIONAL GEOGRAPHIC
LEARNING

Australia • Brazil • Mexico • Singapore • United Kingdom • United States

NATIONAL GEOGRAPHIC
L E A R N I N G

Pathways 1A: Listening, Speaking, and Critical Thinking, 2nd Edition

Becky Tarver Chase

Publisher: Sherrise Roehr

Executive Editor: Laura Le Dréan

Managing Editor: Jennifer Monaghan

Associate Development Editor: Lisl Bove

Associate Development Editor: Jennifer Williams-Rapa

Director of Global and U.S. Marketing: Ian Martin

Product Marketing Manager: Tracy Bailie

Media Research: Leila Hishmeh

Senior Director, Production: Michael Burggren

Manager, Production: Daisy Sosa

Content Project Manager: Mark Rzeszutek

Senior Digital Product Manager: Scott Rule

Manufacturing Planner: Mary Beth Hennebury

Interior and Cover Design: Brenda Carmichael

Art Director: Brenda Carmichael

Composition: MPS North America LLC

For product information and technology assistance, contact us at
Cengage Learning Customer & Sales Support, cengage.com/contact
For permission to use material from this text or product,
submit all requests online at **cengage.com/permissions**
Further permissions questions can be emailed to
permissionrequest@cengage.com

Split 1A Student Edition: 978-1-337-56237-9
Split 1A + Online Workbook: 978-1-337-56255-3

National Geographic Learning
20 Channel Center Street
Boston, MA 02210
USA

National Geographic Learning, a Cengage Learning Company, has a mission to bring the world to the classroom and the classroom to life. With our English language programs, students learn about their world by experiencing it. Through our partnerships with National Geographic and TED Talks, students develop the language and skills they need to be successful global citizens and leaders.

Locate your local office at **international.cengage.com/region**

Visit National Geographic Learning online at **NGL.Cengage.com/ELT**
Visit our corporate website at **www.cengage.com**

Printed in Mexico

Print Number: 04 Print Year: 2022

Contents

Scope and Sequence

Speaking & Presentation	Vocabulary	Grammar & Pronunciation	Critical Thinking
• Communicating that You Don't Understand • Introducing Yourself **Lesson Task** Taking a Career Aptitude Test **Final Task** Speaking about Yourself	Recognizing Word Families	• The Simple Present vs. the Present Continuous • Syllable Stress	**Focus** Evaluating Options Analyzing, Evaluating, Interpreting an Infographic, Making Inferences, Personalizing, Predicting, Prior Knowledge, Reflecting
• Showing Interest • Speaking to a Group **Lesson Task** Discussing Fun Activities **Final Task** Presenting on a Celebration or Holiday	Noun Suffixes	• The Simple Present in *Yes/No* and *Wh-* Questions • Intonation of *Yes/No* and *Wh-* Questions	**Focus** Making Predictions Brainstorming, Organizing Ideas, Personalizing, Prior Knowledge, Ranking, Reflecting
• Clarifying • Ending Strong **Lesson Task** Discussing a Timeline **Final Task** Presenting a Marketing Plan	Common Verb Suffixes	• The Simple Past • Simple Past *-ed* Endings	**Focus** Applying Information Analyzing, Applying, Brainstorming, Interpreting an Infographic, Organizing Ideas, Personalizing, Synthesizing
• Expressing Likes and Dislikes • Making Eye Contact **Lesson Task** Discussing Travel Plans **Final Task** Discussing Ways to Reduce Greenhouse Gases	Words with Similar Meanings	• Count and Noncount Nouns • Reduced *of*	**Focus** Activating Prior Knowledge Analyzing, Analyzing Visuals, Applying, Personalizing, Predicting, Ranking, Reflecting
• Telling a Story with Time Markers • Using an Effective Hook **Lesson Task** Conducting a Survey about Food **Final Task** Presenting a Plan to Stop Food Waste	Recognizing Parts of Speech	• Descriptive Adjectives • Sentence Stress	**Focus** Analyzing Visuals Evaluating, Organizing Ideas, Personalizing, Reflecting

Pathways Listening, Speaking, and Critical Thinking, Second Edition
uses compelling National Geographic stories, photos, video, and
infographics to bring the world to the classroom. Authentic, relevant
content and carefully sequenced lessons engage learners while
equipping them with the skills needed for academic success.

Explore the Theme
provides a visual
introduction to
the unit, engaging
learners academically
and encouraging
them to share ideas
about the unit theme.

D Read the statements and choose T for *True* or F for *False*. The statements were not
stated directly, but you can infer or guess whether they are true or false.

CRITICAL THINKING:
MAKING INFERENCES

1. Annie Griffiths likes her life of adventure.   T   F

2. Griffiths knows how to make friends with strangers.   T   F

3. Griffiths does not mind going to places that are dangerous.   T   F

4. Griffiths' children do not like to travel.   T   F

NEW Integrated listening and speaking activities help **prepare
students for standardized tests** such as IELTS and TOEFL.

UPDATED *Video* sections use relevant National
Geographic **video clips** to give learners another
perspective on the unit theme and further practice of
listening and critical thinking skills.

VOCABULARY SKILL Collocations with Prepositions

Collocations are words that are frequently used together. Prepositions are often used in combination with verbs and nouns and even other prepositions. It is helpful to learn these words together.

ahead of/for	hunt … for	respect for	share with
depend on	relationship with	responsibility for/to	within an hour/a week/5 years

NEW *Vocabulary Skills* help students develop essential word building tools such as understanding collocations, word forms, and connotation.

Listening passages incorporate a variety of listening types such as podcasts, lectures, interviews, and conversations.

NEW *Slide shows* for selected listening passages integrate text and visuals to give learners a more authentic listening experience.

UPDATED Explicit listening skill instruction and practice prepares students to listen and take notes in academic settings.

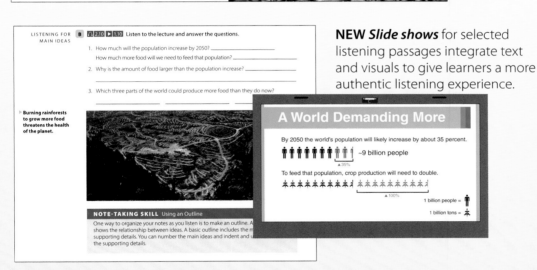

Speaking lessons guide learners from controlled practice to a final speaking task while reinforcing speaking skills, grammar for speaking, and key pronunciation points.

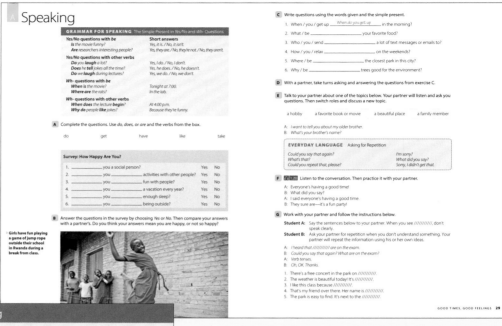

PRESENTATION SKILL Ending Strong

A strong conclusion reminds your listeners of your main ideas and encourages them to think about your presentation after it is over. To end strong, you can:
- summarize and restate your main points.
  As I said, my product is the best on the market because …
- make a connection between your audience and your ideas.
  This service is ideal for you because …
- suggest an action to your audience.
  Look for my product in your local store!

Presentation skills such as starting strong, using specific details, making eye contact, pausing, and summarizing, help learners develop confidence and fluency in communicating ideas.

A ***Final Task*** allows learners to consolidate their understanding of content, language, and skills as they collaborate on an academic presentation.

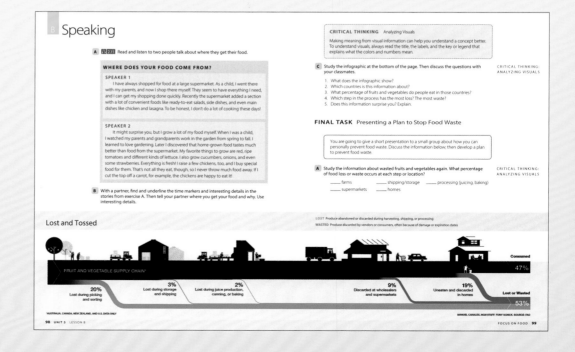

LIVING FOR WORK

1

Artist Todd Stone works on his paintings of the city from his temporary studio on the 67th floor of the World Trade Center in New York, U.S.A.

THINK AND DISCUSS

1 Look at the photo and read the caption. What training or education is needed for this job? What skills are needed?

2 Would you like to do this job? Explain.

3 Read the title of this unit. What do you think it means?

EXPLORE THE THEME

Look at the photo and read the information. Then discuss the questions.

1. What are *millennials*? What ideas do you have about them as a group?

2. Where do millennials work the most hours? The least?

3. Is any of this information surprising to you? Explain.

4. Does this office seem like a good place to work? Why or why not?

MILLENNIALS AT WORK

WHERE DO MILLENNIALS WORK THE LONGEST HOURS?

Average number of hours worked each week by people aged 20-34

India	52
Mexico	48
China	48
Singapore	48
Greece	47
Japan	46
United States	45
Brazil	45
France	44
Spain	43
Germany	43
Italy	43
Canada	42
Australia	41
United Kingdom	41

A Vocabulary

A 🎧 **1.2** Read and listen to the words. Then match each word with its definition.

1. __c__ ordinary
2. _____ opportunity
3. _____ experiences
4. _____ skills
5. _____ dangerous

a. (n) a chance to do something
b. (adj) likely to cause harm or injury
c. (adj) common, regular
d. (n) things you do or that happen to you
e. (n) things you are able to do well

MEANING FROM CONTEXT

B 🎧 **1.3** Look at the photo and read the caption. Then listen to the article. Notice each word in **blue** and think about its meaning.

▶ **Dereck and Beverly Joubert photographing a meerkat in Africa**

Beverly and Dereck Joubert

Beverly Joubert and her husband Dereck are **creative** people. Together, they write and make interesting films about animals in Africa. In order to work together, they need to **communicate** well and understand one another.

They love to **explore** different parts of Africa. Making films there is an **adventure**. Big cats such as lions are some of their **favorite** animals, so they make films and raise money to help them. Their Big Cats Initiative program provides money so that more than 100 conservationists can work in the field to help save the big cats.

C Write each word in **blue** from exercise B next to its definition.

1. ___creative___ (adj) having imagination and artistic ability
2. _____ (v) to go to different places and learn about things
3. _____ (n) an exciting time or event
4. _____ (v) to share information with others
5. _____ (adj) preferred, most liked

VOCABULARY SKILL Recognizing Word Families

Word families include words with the same root but different forms. For example, *explore* is a verb with the root *explor-*. The noun form, *exploration*, has the same root, but the ending *-ation* makes it a noun. The adjective form, *exploratory*, adds the ending *-atory* to the root. Expand your vocabulary by learning more than one form when you learn a new word.

D Work with a partner. Complete the chart with other forms of these words from exercises A and B. You can use a dictionary to help you.

Noun	Verb	Adjective
exploration	explore	exploratory
	communicate	
experience		
		creative

E 🎧 **1.4** Read the article and fill in each blank with a word from the box. Then listen and check your answers.

| adventure | experiences | favorite | ordinary | skills |

Photographer Annie Griffiths

Annie Griffiths is famous for her beautiful photographs. She travels all over the world to take photos. Living in other countries is not for everyone, but for Griffiths and her children, it's an _____. One of her children's
1
_____ places is the Middle East. Their
2
_____ in that part of the world helped
3
them to learn about other cultures.

Griffiths' work is often exciting. In the Galápagos Islands, she found herself in the water with sharks one day! But most of the time she is with _____ people.
4

Besides writing and taking pictures, Griffiths teaches photography _____
5
to people who want to become photographers. They know they are learning from one of the best photographers in the world.

Annie Griffiths on location in Petra, Jordan

Listening An Interview with Annie Griffiths

BEFORE LISTENING

CRITICAL THINKING:
PREDICTING

A You are going to listen to an interview with National Geographic photographer Annie Griffiths. Look at the photo and read the information. What do you think Griffiths will talk about? Discuss your ideas with a partner.

About My Photo

Where: Victoria Falls, Zambia   When: around sunset, in 2006

What: a swimmer   Why: beautiful light, amazing place

WHILE LISTENING

> **LISTENING SKILL** Identifying Main Ideas
>
> Identifying a speaker's main ideas will help you focus your listening and understand more of what you hear. The main ideas are the speaker's most important points. When you listen for main ideas, you focus on the gist, or central topic. Details support the main ideas and can include examples, reasons, explanations, and additional information.
>
> **Main idea:** *Annie Griffiths is famous for her beautiful photographs.*
>
> **Detail:** *The photos are of places all over the world.*

LISTENING FOR
MAIN IDEAS

B 🎧 1.5 ▶ 1.1 Listen to the interview with Annie Griffiths. Check (✓) the main idea of the interview.

☐ Annie Griffiths' work is dangerous sometimes.
☐ Annie Griffiths travels around the world as a photographer.
☐ Annie Griffiths knows how to communicate with the people she meets.

C 🎧 1.5 Listen again and take notes on important details. Use only key words and phrases.   NOTE TAKING

1. Her favorite places: _____ S. Africa, Galápagos Isl., Mex. _____

2. Why she loves to travel: _____

3. Why she took her children: _____

4. How she communicates: _____

5. Skills needed to be a photographer: _____

AFTER LISTENING

D Read the statements and choose T for *True* or F for *False*. The statements were not stated directly, but you can infer or guess whether they are true or false.   CRITICAL THINKING: MAKING INFERENCES

1. Annie Griffiths likes her life of adventure.   T   F

2. Griffiths knows how to make friends with strangers.   T   F

3. Griffiths does not mind going to places that are dangerous.   T   F

4. Griffiths' children do not like to travel.   T   F

E Discuss the questions below with a partner.   CRITICAL THINKING: REFLECTING

1. Griffiths takes her children to work. Is it a good idea to take your family to work?
2. What places do you like to travel to? What do you think is fun and interesting about traveling?

◀ **Annie Griffiths' children in Petra, Jordan, wearing Bedouin clothing and pretending to drink tea**

A Speaking

GRAMMAR FOR SPEAKING The Simple Present vs. the Present Continuous

We use the **simple present** to express:

1. repeated actions or habits: *He **goes** to work at 8:00 every day.*

2. actions or states that are always true: *Photographers **take** pictures.*

Note: We use the simple present with adverbs of frequency (*never, rarely, occasionally, sometimes, often, usually, always*) to say how often we do things.

We use the **present continuous** to express:

1. actions happening now: *She **is taking** a photo.*

2. actions happening around this time: *I **am traveling** a lot these days.*

Note: We use the present continuous with expressions like *now, right now,* and *at this moment.*

A Read the conversations below. Fill in each blank with the simple present or the present continuous form of a verb from the box. You will use one verb twice. Then practice each conversation with a partner.

cook	help	sell	show	work	write

A: What do you do for work?

B: I _____ work _____ in a restaurant.
   ₁

A: What are you doing right now?

B: I _____ a new meal for tonight.
   ₂

A: It smells delicious.

A: Hi! What are you working on?

B: I _____ a new computer program.
   ₃

A: Sounds interesting.

A: You're a real estate agent, right?

B: Yes, that's right. I _____ and _____ homes.
   ₄   ₅

   I _____ a house to a buyer this morning.
   ₆

A: What do you do for your job?

B: I'm a police officer. I _____ people who are in trouble.
   ₇

King's Cross Railway
Station in the U.K.

B Work with a partner. Answer the questions and discuss different jobs.

In what job do you   ... help people?
                        ... explore different places?
                        ... need good communication skills?
                        ... travel a lot?
                        ... need special skills?

A: *Police officers help people.*
B: *Right. Teachers do, too.*

C Work with your partner. Look at the photo and discuss what the people are doing.

D Work with your partner. Follow the instructions below.

1. Look around the room. Talk about three things that are happening in the room now.
2. Think of someone you know well. Tell your partner three things that person is probably doing right now.
3. Think of a job you both know about. Make a list of three things a person with that job does every day.

E Work with a partner. Read the work schedule of a hotel housekeeper named Erica. Then answer the questions below.

1. Which days does Erica work at the hotel? Which days does she not work?
2. Which day is Erica's longest workday? Which is the shortest?
3. What does Erica have to do for her job?

Hotel Avalon

Weekly work schedule: Erica S.

Tuesday	Wednesday	Thursday	Friday	Saturday
start: 7:00 a.m.	start: 7:00 a.m.	start: 7:00 a.m.	start: 7:00 a.m.	start: 7:00 a.m.
				end: 12:00 p.m.
end: 3:30 p.m.	end: 3:30 p.m.		end: 3:30 p.m.	
		end: 5:30 p.m.		

Job Duties:
Every day: clean the guest bathrooms; make beds; remove trash
Tuesday through Friday: get clean sheets and towels from the hotel laundry room
Wednesday and Friday: clean the dining room after breakfast
Saturday: put new menus and information cards in the guest rooms

F With your partner, discuss Erica's weekly schedule using adverbs of frequency. Use the information from exercise E and your own ideas.

A: *Erica always starts work early in the morning.*
B: *Erica never works in the hotel kitchen.*

G Form a small group. Discuss which of these words you might use to describe Erica's job. Then think of two more words that describe her job.

dangerous   difficult   easy   high-paying   interesting   physical

H Work with a partner. Discuss your weekly schedules. Use the questions below and your own ideas.

1. Which days do you work? What time do you start and end?
2. Which days do you go to school? Which day is your longest school day?
3. What are some things you do often each week? Sometimes? Rarely?
4. What are you doing right after class today?
5. What are you doing a lot these days?

LESSON TASK Taking a Career Aptitude Test

A Work with a partner. Take turns asking and answering the questions from the Career Aptitude Test. Take short notes on your partner's answers.

Career Aptitude Test	
A career aptitude test can help you decide which job or career is right for you.	
Interview Questions	**My Partner's Answers**
1. Are you a creative person?	
2. Do you like to travel and explore new places?	
3. Are you afraid of dangerous situations, for example, working with animals or with electricity?	
4. Do you have good communication skills?	
5. Do you like to spend time with other people, or do you prefer to spend time alone?	
6. Do you like to keep fit?	
7. Are you a good problem solver?	
8. Do you like to help people?	
9. Do you like to do a lot of different things every day?	
10. Which is more important to you in a job: adventure or money?	

B Look back at your notes from exercise A. Then tell your partner which jobs in the box below might be good for him or her. Explain your reasons.

business executive	doctor/nurse	firefighter	photographer	salesperson
computer programmer	farmer	news reporter	restaurant worker	teacher

C Form a group with another pair of students and follow the steps below.

1. Tell the group which job might be best for your partner. Explain your reasons.
2. Tell the group your opinion of your partner's choice of job for you. Is it really a good job for you? Why or why not?

Video

Students set the table before a formal dinner at The International Butler Academy in Chengdu, China.

Becoming a Butler

BEFORE VIEWING

PRIOR KNOWLEDGE

A Look at the photo and think about what you know about butlers. Mark each statement T for *True* or F for *False*. Compare your ideas with a partner.

1. Butlers usually work in England.   T   F

2. Butlers work for rich people in large houses.   T   F

3. Butlers wear informal clothes.   T   F

4. Butlers speak in a formal way.   T   F

B Match each word from the video to its definition. Use your dictionary to help you.

1. _____ refreshments   a. (v) to go and get something

2. _____ fetch   b. (v) to do something again and again in order to improve

3. _____ practice   c. (n) a custom or belief that has existed for a long time

4. _____ tradition   d. (n) things to drink or eat

WHILE VIEWING

C ▶ 1.2 Watch the video. Choose the correct word or phrase for each sentence.

UNDERSTANDING MAIN IDEAS

1. In the past, there were (many / few) butlers.
2. Nowadays, there are (many / few) butlers.
3. The students at the school come from (one country / many countries).
4. Butler school is (easy / difficult) for the students.

D ▶ 1.2 Watch the video again. Check (✓) the things students do at the butler school.

UNDERSTANDING DETAILS

☐ graduate from school   ☐ learn to walk correctly

☐ iron newspapers   ☐ practice saying things

☐ learn from books   ☐ wash clothes

AFTER VIEWING

> **CRITICAL THINKING** Evaluating Options
>
> Most options or choices have both good and bad points. When you evaluate options or choices, you judge them based on their value to you. Think about what is most important to you as you consider the pros and cons of your choices.

E Read the list of careers and the pros and cons in the boxes below. Then discuss with a partner, evaluating the options and deciding which career choices could be good for you. Consider the pros and cons in the box and your own ideas.

CRITICAL THINKING: EVALUATING

A: *I think doctors work very long hours.*
B: *That's true, but they make a high salary and money is very important to me.*

Careers	
firefighter	teacher
news reporter	doctor
oceanographer	scientist
businessperson	waiter
photographer	butler

Pros and Cons	
dangerous	travel opportunities
high salary	easy work
low pay	long hours
difficult job	opportunities to learn
interesting work	physically difficult or demanding

B Vocabulary

MEANING FROM
CONTEXT

A 🎧 **1.6** Read and listen to three interviews. Notice each word in **blue** and think about its meaning. Then practice the interviews with a partner.

> **Q:** What kind of people make good nurses?
>
> **A:** Well, you have to be **organized**. For example, I'm **in charge of** my patients' medication, so I write everything down in a chart. It has a big **effect** on my patients' health, so it's important to me.
>
> **Q:** What other skills do you need?
>
> **A:** Nurses also have to be fit because the work is very **physical**. I stand or walk all the time, and sometimes I have to lift patients up from their beds.
> ───
> **Q:** Do you enjoy your volunteer work with that environmental group?
>
> **A:** Yes, I do. **Although** it can be frustrating.
>
> **Q:** Why?
>
> **A:** Well, even though the town passed a clean-air **initiative**, **pollution** is still a problem.
>
> **Q:** But it's getting better, right?
>
> **A:** Yes, it is. And companies are definitely getting better at recycling, too.
> ───
> **Q:** What does an engineer do every day?
>
> **A:** Well, there are many kinds of engineers. I'm an industrial engineer. I look at our processes here at the factory, and I **search** for problems.
>
> **Q:** What do you do if you find a problem?
>
> **A:** I give a **presentation** to my **managers**. I explain the problem to them, and we try to find ways to solve it.

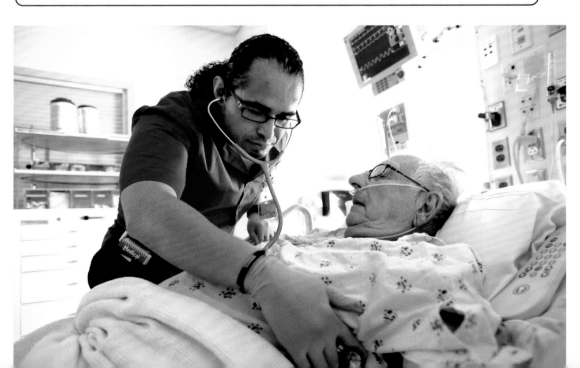

▶ **David Fuentes, a masters student in the nursing program at the University of California, Los Angeles (UCLA), examines a patient.**

B Complete each sentence with a word from the box.

> effect (n)   physical (adj)   pollution (n)   presentations (n)   search (v)

1. Human activity often causes _____. This hurts the environment.
2. Roland needs to _____ for a new job.
3. He speaks well and is good at making business _____.
4. They exercise and they're very fit, so they can do very _____ work.
5. A good manager can have a positive _____ on the employees' work.

C 🎧 **1.7** Read the conversation and fill in each blank with a word or phrase from the box. Then listen and check your answers.

> although (conj)   in charge of (phr)   initiative (n)   manager (n)   organized (adj)

Interviewer:	So, you are applying for the job of office _____ . Why do you think it's right for you?
Applicant:	Well, I'm very _____ . At my last job, we moved offices and I managed the move.
Interviewer:	Can you manage other employees?
Applicant:	Yes. In my last job, I was _____ five other employees. _____ it was hard work, I enjoyed it a lot.
Interviewer:	Great. What other job skills do you have?
Applicant:	I'm a self-starter. I saw that parking was a problem where I worked, so I started a ride-sharing _____ .

D Work with a partner. Role-play the situation below. Then switch roles.

Student A: You are a manager. Ask your partner the job interview questions from the conversation in exercise C.

Student B: You are the applicant at a job interview. You really want the job. Answer the interview questions with your own ideas.

E Discuss the questions below with your partner.

CRITICAL THINKING: REFLECTING

1. What effect does each worker in exercise A have on the world around them? For example, what effect does the nurse have on his patients' health?
2. What does the volunteer say about pollution? Do you think she is right? Explain.
3. Besides nursing, what other jobs are very physical? Are they good jobs, in your opinion?
4. In what ways are you an organized student? How could you be more organized?

Listening A Conversation about Dr. Sylvia Earle

BEFORE LISTENING

> **PRONUNCIATION** Syllable Stress
>
> 🎧 **1.8** We can divide words in English into one or more syllables. For example, *doctor* has two syllables (doc-tor). In words with more than one syllable, one syllable usually receives the main stress. For example, in the word *doctor*, *doc* is stressed. The syllable with the main stress is louder and clearer than the other syllables.
>
> | One syllable | Two syllables | Three syllables |
> |---|---|---|
> | **job** | **doc**-tor | **com**-pa-ny |

A 🎧 **1.9** Listen and mark the main stress in each word.

1. <u>stu</u>dy	3. travel	5. reporter	7. receive
2. nurse	4. remember	6. creative	8. skills

B 🎧 **1.10** Write each word from the box in the correct column of the chart below. Then listen and check your answers.

adventure	cook	know	officer	travel
amazing	fly	money	teacher	yesterday

One syllable	Two syllables	Three syllables
cook	*money*	*adventure*

C 🎧 **1.11** You are going to listen to a conversation between students about oceanographer Sylvia Earle. Here are some words you will hear. Listen and repeat the words. Then answer the questions below.

billion	marine biologist	ocean	pollution	tuna

1. How many syllables are in each word? Write the number of syllables next to each word.
2. Which syllable in each word receives the main stress? Mark the syllables with the main stress.

WHILE LISTENING

D 🎧 **1.12** Listen to the first part of the conversation. What presentation are the students talking about? Check (✓) the correct answer.

☐ one that Becca missed ☐ one that Ren missed ☐ one that was not good

E 🎧 **1.13** Listen to the entire conversation. Check (✓) the main idea.

LISTENING FOR
MAIN IDEAS

☐ Becca was not in class on Thursday because she was sick.

☐ Dr. Earle's presentation was very interesting.

☐ People are having a bad effect on the oceans, but we can change that.

F 🎧 **1.13** Listen again. Check (✓) any ideas that are NOT part of the conversation.

LISTENING FOR
DETAILS

☐ Becca feels better today.

☐ Dr. Earle gave a presentation to the class on Thursday.

☐ Dr. Earle earns a high salary.

☐ There are more than seven billion people on earth now.

☐ Dr. Earle doesn't eat fish.

Dr. Sylvia Earle

AFTER LISTENING

G Read each statement and choose *Agree* or *Disagree* for each.

PERSONALIZING

1. Dr. Earle's career might be a good career for me.   Agree   Disagree
2. When you're sick, it's better not to go to class.   Agree   Disagree
3. The large number of people in the world is a problem.   Agree   Disagree
4. What people eat has a big effect on the oceans.   Agree   Disagree

> **EVERYDAY LANGUAGE**   Showing that You're Listening
>
> Use these expressions to show someone that you're listening and interested in the conversation.
>
> *Really?*   *I see.*   *Interesting!*   *Um-hmm.*   *I see your point.*   *Wow!*

H Form a small group. Discuss the statements in exercise G. Give reasons why you agree or disagree with each statement. Use the expressions from the box to show interest in your classmates' ideas.

B Speaking

> **SPEAKING SKILL** Communicating that You Don't Understand
>
> Here are some expressions to communicate that you don't understand what someone says.
>
> *I don't understand.* *I'm sorry?* *I'm not sure what you mean.*
> *Do you mean . . . ?* *Can you explain?* *I'm not sure I follow.*

A 🎧 **1.14** Read and listen to the conversation. Then <u>underline</u> the expressions that show when the speakers don't understand.

> A: What's your major?
>
> B: Marine biology.
>
> A: I'm sorry?
>
> B: Marine biology. It's the study of marine organisms and their ecosystems.
>
> A: Do you mean you study fish and other forms of life in the ocean?
>
> B: Exactly.
>
> A: And what can you do with that?
>
> B: I'm not sure what you mean.
>
> A: What jobs can you get?
>
> B: Oh, gosh, a lot of different things. I can do research or teach; I could be a fisheries biologist . . .
>
> A: Stop there. Fisheries? What are those?
>
> B: They raise fish. And there's also aquaculture . . .

B Practice the conversation from exercise A with a partner. Then switch roles and practice it again.

C Practice the conversations below with your partner. Student B uses one of the expressions from the box. Then switch roles and practice the conversations again using different expressions.

1. A: You need a lot of special skills to be a marine biologist.

    B: . . .

    A: Well, to study the ocean, you need to know how to do many things.

2. A: Working in tourism is an adventure.

    B: . . .

    A: Every day you meet people from different places and cultures.

D Work with a partner. Look at the infographic. Then answer the questions below.

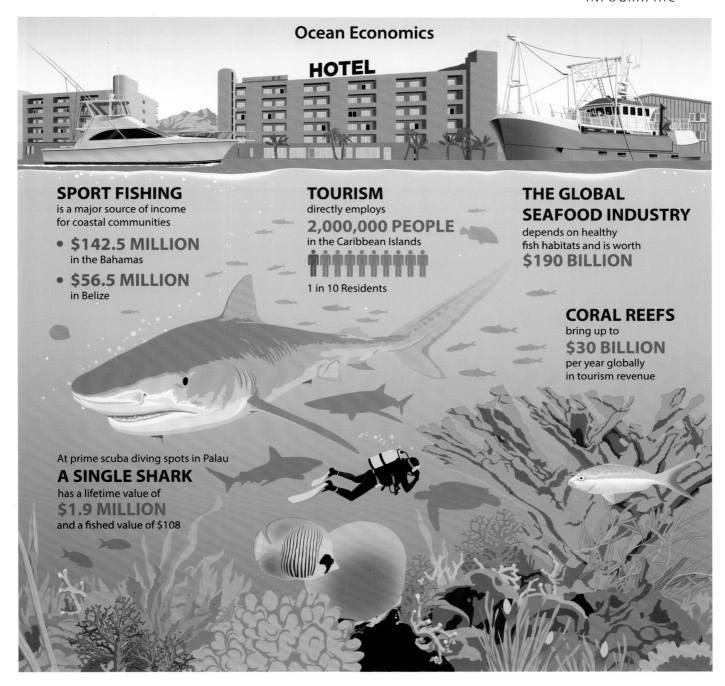

Ocean Economics

HOTEL

SPORT FISHING
is a major source of income
for coastal communities

- **$142.5 MILLION**
  in the Bahamas
- **$56.5 MILLION**
  in Belize

At prime scuba diving spots in Palau
A SINGLE SHARK
has a lifetime value of
$1.9 MILLION
and a fished value of $108

TOURISM
directly employs
2,000,000 PEOPLE
in the Caribbean Islands

1 in 10 Residents

**THE GLOBAL
SEAFOOD INDUSTRY**
depends on healthy
fish habitats and is worth
$190 BILLION

CORAL REEFS
bring up to
$30 BILLION
per year globally
in tourism revenue

1. How many people in the Caribbean Islands does tourism employ?
2. Which is more valuable: a shark attracting scuba divers or a shark as food?
3. Why are healthy fish habitats important to the ocean economy?
4. What do you think is the purpose of this infographic?
5. What question(s) would you like answered after looking at this information?

E With a partner, list as many jobs as you can that might benefit from healthy coastal communities and coral reefs. Use the infographic for ideas.

FINAL TASK Speaking about Yourself

> You are going to give a short presentation about yourself. You will introduce yourself and share what job you hope to have.

ORGANIZING IDEAS **A** Write answers to the questions below in your notebook. Then share them with a partner.

1. What's your name *(the name you want to be called in this class)*?
2. Where are you from?
3. What subjects are you studying?
4. What job do you have or hope to have in the future? Why?

PRESENTATION SKILL Introducing Yourself

When you give a presentation, you can use these expressions to introduce yourself.

> Hi, I'm (your name)./Hello, my name is (your name).
> I'm from (your city, country, university, etc.).

B 🎧 1.15 Read and listen to one student's presentation. Then follow the steps below.

> *Hi, everyone. My name is Alejandro, but please call me Alex. I'm from Bogotá. As you probably know, that's the capital city of Colombia. I'm studying English now, and I'm also studying international relations. I hope to work for an international aid organization someday. I want to travel the world, and I want to help people, too, so I think this is a good job for me.*

1. Underline the expressions Alex uses to introduce himself.
2. Circle the reasons Alex gives for the job he wants.
3. Decide which expressions you will use to introduce yourself.

PRESENTING **C** Introduce yourself to your classmates. Then tell them about yourself using the information from exercise A.

REFLECTION

1. Which skill in this unit do you think will help you the most?

   _____

   _____

2. Which of the jobs mentioned in this unit sounds the most interesting to you? Why?

   _____

   _____

3. Here are the vocabulary words from the unit. Check (✔) the ones you can use.

☐ adventure	☐ explore	☐ organized
☐ although	☐ favorite	☐ physical AWL
☐ communicate AWL	☐ in charge of	☐ pollution
☐ creative AWL	☐ initiative AWL	☐ presentation
☐ dangerous	☐ manager	☐ search
☐ effect	☐ opportunity	☐ skill
☐ experience	☐ ordinary	

GOOD TIMES, GOOD FEELINGS 2

Hundreds of people practice yoga beneath Singapore's Supertrees.

THINK AND DISCUSS

1 Look at the photo. Why do you think all these people are doing yoga here? How do you think they feel?

2 Read the unit title. What do you do to feel good?

Look at the map and read the information. Then discuss the questions.

1. What is HPI? How is it measured?

2. Which country ranks the happiest?

3. According to the map, which continent has the most "happy" countries?

4. According to the chart, which is better: a high or low environmental footprint? A high or low percentage of inequality?

5. What do you think is the most interesting or surprising information presented?

HAPPY PLANET INDEX

TOP 15 COUNTRIES

Rank /140	Country	HPI	♥	☺	👣	⚖
1st	Costa Rica	47.7	79.1	7.3	2.8	15%
2nd	Mexico	40.7	76.4	7.3	2.9	19%
3rd	Colombia	40.7	73.7	6.4	1.9	24%
4th	Vanuatu	40.6	71.3	6.5	1.9	22%
5th	Vietnam	40.3	75.5	5.5	1.7	19%
6th	Panama	39.5	77.2	6.9	2.8	19%
7th	Nicaragua	38.4	74.3	5.4	1.4	25%
8th	Bangladesh	38.4	70.8	4.7	0.7	27%
9th	Thailand	37.3	74.1	6.3	2.7	15%
10th	Ecuador	37.0	75.4	6.0	2.2	22%
11th	Jamaica	36.9	75.3	5.6	1.9	21%
12th	Norway	36.8	81.3	7.7	5.0	7%
13th	Albania	36.8	77.3	5.5	2.2	17%
14th	Uruguay	36.1	76.9	6.4	2.9	18%
15th	Spain	36.0	82.2	6.3	3.7	10%

KEY

Highest — Lowest

HPI Happy Planet Index score:

♥ Life Expectancy (years)

☺ Wellbeing (out of 10)

👣 Environmental Footprint (global hectares/person)

⚖ Inequality (%)

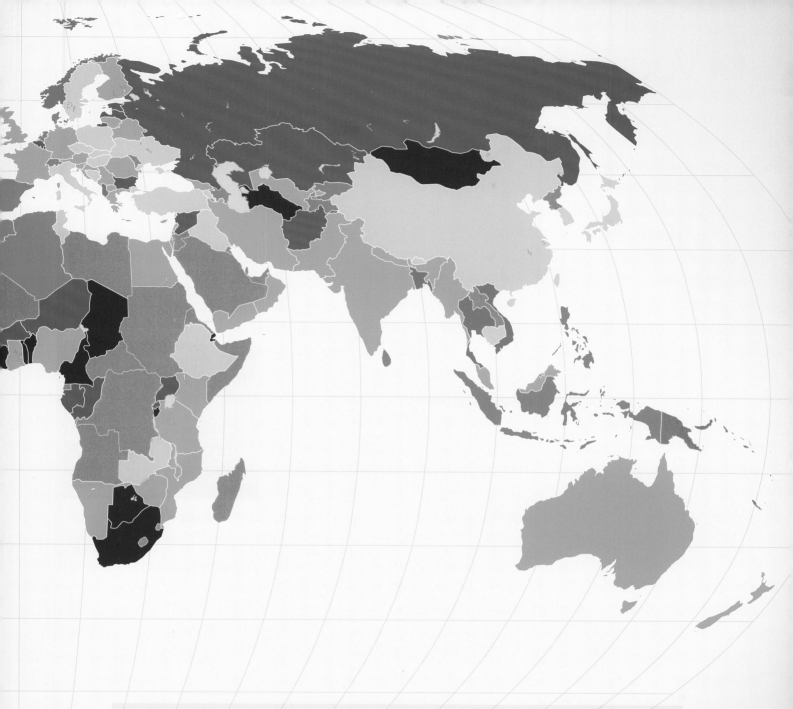

How do you measure the happiness of a country? In 2016, the Happy Planet Index (HPI) was created to look at 140 countries around the world to see where people are living the longest and happiest lives with the least impact on the planet. The HPI combines four factors:

- life expectancy (the average number of years a person is expected to live)
- overall wellbeing (people's satisfaction on a scale of 0 to 10)
- environmental footprint (each person's impact on the planet)
- inequality (a percentage showing how uneven life is for different people within a country)

A Vocabulary

A 🎧 **1.16** Listen and check (✓) the words you already know. Use a dictionary to help you with any new words.

☐ amusing (adj)   ☐ joke (n)   ☐ recorded (v)   ☐ sound (n)
☐ comedy (n)   ☐ laughter (n)   ☐ researcher (n)
☐ happiness (n)   ☐ led (v)   ☐ situations (n)

MEANING FROM CONTEXT

B 🎧 **1.17** Read and listen to the article. Notice each word in **blue** and think about its meaning.

FROM PANT-PANT TO HA-HA

A chimpanzee

Look at the photo. Does this look like laughter? New research says that apes laugh when they are tickled. A **researcher** at the University of Portsmouth in the U.K. **led** a "tickle team." The team tickled the necks, feet, hands, and armpits of young apes. The team **recorded** more than 800 of the resulting laughs on tape. The research suggests that the apes' panting noise is the **sound** of **laughter**. Researchers think that this short, quick breathing is the starting point of human expressions of **happiness**—the "ha-ha" sound we make when we laugh. When we find something **amusing**, such as a **joke**, we laugh. When apes find something amusing, such as a tickle, they laugh. Humans find many **situations** funny—such as jokes, tickles, TV **comedy** shows—but we are not unique because animals laugh, too.

C Write each word in **blue** from exercise B next to its definition below.

1. ___amusing___ causing laughter or pleasure
2. _____ a funny movie, play, show, or story
3. _____ a noise; something that can be heard
4. _____ a person who studies or investigates something scientifically
5. _____ great pleasure
6. _____ directed, showed the way
7. _____ a thing that someone says to make people laugh
8. _____ made an audio or written copy of something
9. _____ the sound of happiness or amusement
10. _____ how things are at certain times and places

D Complete each sentence with a word from exercise C. Use each word only once. Then practice the exchanges with a partner.

1. A: Social ___situations___ such as parties sometimes make me nervous.
   B: Me, too.

2. A: They felt great _____ when they held their first grandchild.
   B: I'm sure they were really pleased.

3. A: So, who _____ the group discussion yesterday?
   B: Adriana did. She asked some really good questions about the topic.

4. A: There is a new _____ on Professor Watson's team.
   B: Interesting. What is she studying?

5. A: Larry told a _____ but it wasn't _____. Nobody even smiled.
   B: Poor Larry!

6. A: They must be having fun. I hear _____ coming from next door.
   B: Yeah, they're watching their favorite _____ show.

7. A: I missed the lecture.
   B: Don't worry. I _____ it on my computer. We can listen to it again later.

8. A: Your car is making a really odd _____.
   B: Really? Maybe I should take it to a mechanic.

VOCABULARY SKILL Noun Suffixes

When you see or hear a word you don't know, recognizing the part of speech can help you understand its meaning. Some suffixes, or word endings, are very common for nouns: *-er/-or/-ar, -ion, -tion, -sion, -ness, -ence/-ance*.

Verb	Noun
teach	teacher
create	creation
decide	decision

E With a partner, answer the questions below using the noun form of the word in bold.

1. What do you call a person who **researches** a subject?
2. If you are **happy**, what feeling do you have?
3. In most groups, there is one or more people who **lead** and the rest **follow**. What do you call these two types of people?
4. What is the sound people make when they laugh?

F Discuss the questions below in a small group.   PERSONALIZING

1. When was the last time you laughed a lot? What was so amusing?
2. What do you do that makes other people laugh?
3. What situations do you find amusing?

> *My friend tells jokes. The jokes are so bad I laugh!*

A Listening A Lecture about Laughter

BEFORE LISTENING

> **CRITICAL THINKING** Making Predictions
>
> When you make predictions about content, it helps you focus your listening. Use your experience and knowledge to predict what you will hear. Ask yourself questions such as:
>
> *What will I listen to—a lecture, a conversation, an interview?*
> *What will it be about? What can I predict based on the title or the topic?*
> *Who will speak? What do I know about the speaker(s)?*

CRITICAL THINKING:
PREDICTING

A You are going to hear a lecture about laughter. With your partner, check (✓) what you think you will hear.

☐ two people talking   ☐ facts about laughter
☐ examples of jokes   ☐ research results

WHILE LISTENING

> **LISTENING SKILL** Understanding the Speaker's Purpose
>
> You will understand more if you know *why* a speaker is giving a talk, lecture, etc. This is the speaker's purpose. Often you must guess the speaker's purpose based on what they say and how they say it. But sometimes speakers will state their purpose directly:
>
> **I'm here today to** *explain the importance of play.*
> **My goal today is to** *teach you three new jokes.*

B 🎧 1.18 Read the questions and answers below. Then listen to the first part of the lecture and choose the correct answers.

1. What is the speaker's main purpose?

   a. to make us laugh   b. to give us information

2. Does the speaker directly state her purpose?

   a. yes   b. no

CHECKING
PREDICTIONS

C 🎧 1.19 ▶ 1.3 Look back at the predictions you made in exercise A. Then listen to the entire lecture. Which of your predictions were correct?

🎧 1.19 Read the statements and answer choices below. Then listen again and choose the best word or phrase to complete each statement.

1. People usually laugh _____.
   a. at good jokes
   b. after they learn to talk
   c. when other people laugh

2. People will probably *not* laugh _____.
   a. in a social situation
   b. when they're with friends
   c. when they're alone

E 🎧 1.19 Read the statements. Then listen again and complete each statement with information from the lecture.

1. Professor Panksepp, the rat researcher, works at _____ State University.

2. The rats' laughter is at a very _____ frequency, so people can't hear it.

3. More than _____ percent of laughter is *not* because of jokes.

4. TV comedy shows often use a _____ track to make the audience laugh.

AFTER LISTENING

F Discuss the questions below with a partner.

1. Do you think it's a good idea to use animals for research? Explain.
2. Do you think some people laugh more than others? If so, what do you think the reason is for this?
3. Is it always a good thing to laugh? Are there times when it is not good to laugh? Explain.

Professor Panksepp studied rats to learn why animals laugh.

Speaking

GRAMMAR FOR SPEAKING The Simple Present in *Yes/No* and *Wh-* Questions

Yes/No questions with be	**Short answers**
Is the movie funny?	*Yes, it is. / No, it isn't.*
Are researchers interesting people?	*Yes, they are. / No, they're not. / No, they aren't.*
Yes/No questions with other verbs	
Do you **laugh** a lot?	*Yes, I do. / No, I don't.*
Does he **tell** jokes all the time?	*Yes, he does. / No, he doesn't.*
Do we **laugh** during lectures?	*Yes, we do. / No, we don't.*
Wh- questions with be	
When is the movie?	*Tonight at 7:00.*
Where are the rats?	*In the lab.*
Wh- questions with other verbs	
When does the lecture **begin**?	*At 4:00 p.m.*
Why do people **like** jokes?	*Because they're funny.*

A Complete the questions. Use *do* or *are* and the verbs from the box.

do	get	have	like	take

Survey: How Happy Are You?

1. _____ you a social person?		Yes	No
2. _____ you _____ activities with other people?		Yes	No
3. _____ you _____ fun with people?		Yes	No
4. _____ you _____ a vacation every year?		Yes	No
5. _____ you _____ enough sleep?		Yes	No
6. _____ you _____ being outside?		Yes	No

B Answer the questions in the survey by choosing *Yes* or *No*. Then compare your answers with a partner's. Do you think your answers mean you are happy, or not so happy?

▶ **Girls have fun playing a game of jump rope outside their school in Rwanda during a break from class.**

C Write questions using the words given and the simple present.

1. When / you / get up ___When do you get up___ in the morning?

2. What / be _____ your favorite food?

3. Who / you / send _____ a lot of text messages or emails to?

4. How / you / relax _____ on the weekends?

5. Where / be _____ the closest park in this city?

6. Why / be _____ trees good for the environment?

D With a partner, take turns asking and answering the questions from exercise C.

E Talk to your partner about one of the topics below. Your partner will listen and ask you questions. Then switch roles and discuss a new topic.

| a hobby | a favorite book or movie | a beautiful place | a family member |

A: *I want to tell you about my older brother.*
B: *What's your brother's name?*

EVERYDAY LANGUAGE Asking for Repetition

Could you say that again?   *I'm sorry?*
What's that?   *What did you say?*
Could you repeat that, please?   *Sorry, I didn't get that.*

F 🎧 1.20 **Listen to the conversation. Then practice it with your partner.**

A: Everyone's having a good time!
B: What did you say?
A: I said everyone's having a good time.
B: They sure are—it's a fun party!

G Work with your partner and follow the instructions below.

Student A: Say the sentences below to your partner. When you see ///////////, don't speak clearly.

Student B: Ask your partner for repetition when you don't understand something. Your partner will repeat the information using his or her own ideas.

A: *I heard that ////////// are on the exam.*
B: *Could you say that again? What are on the exam?*
A: *Verb tenses.*
B: *Oh, OK. Thanks.*

1. There's a free concert in the park on ///////////.
2. The weather is beautiful today! It's ///////////.
3. I like this class because ///////////.
4. That's my friend over there. Her name is ///////////.
5. The park is easy to find. It's next to the ///////////.

PRONUNCIATION Intonation of Yes/No and Wh- Questions

🎧 1.21 Intonation is the rise and fall of your voice. When you ask a *yes/no* question, your voice rises or goes up on the last content word. Content words are adjectives, adverbs, nouns, and verbs.

Do you think it's **funny**?   *Is she really* **laughing**?

When you ask a *wh-* question, your voice rises on the stressed syllable of the last content word, and then falls at the end of the question.

Where is the nearest **park**?   *When are you* **going**?

H 🎧 1.22 Read the two conversations. Mark the intonation you think you will hear in the questions. Then listen and check your answers. Practice the conversations with a partner. Then switch roles and practice them again.

Conversation 1	Conversation 2
A: What's the name of the park?	A: Do you like to go to the park?
B: It's called the High Line.	B: Yes, I do. I go there to run.
A: Is it in New York City?	A: Why do you do that?
B: Yes, it is.	B: It's good exercise, and I enjoy being outdoors.
A: Why do people go there?	A: Are you going again tomorrow?
B: It's a good place to relax.	B: Yes. Do you want to come?

I Take turns asking your partner *yes/no* and *wh-* questions about what he or she does to have fun.

dance	go to parties	watch TV	socialize with friends	play games

A: *Do you like to dance?*
B: *No, I don't. Do you?*
A: *Yes, I do! What do you like to do instead?*
B: *I like to socialize with my friends.*

J Form a small group. One member of the group thinks of a well-known TV show or movie. Other members of the group ask *yes/no* questions to find out the name of the show or movie.

A: *Is it a movie?*
B: *No, it's a TV show.*
C: *Does this show come on at the same time every week?*
B: *Yes, it does.*
A: *Do older people like to watch this show?*

LESSON TASK Discussing Fun Activities

A Think of an activity you enjoy. Read the questions. Complete the chart with your answers.

	My Answers	My Partner's Answers
1. What's the activity?		
2. How often do you do it?		
3. When do you do it?		
4. Who do you do it with?		
5. Do you have to wear special clothes?		
6. What do you do?		
7. Where does it take place?		
8. Why do you like it?		
9.		

B With a partner, ask and answer the questions in exercise A. Complete the chart. Add one more question to find out more about your partner's activity.

C Form a group with another pair of students. Report what you learned about your partner in exercise B.

The High Line is an elevated park on an old railway in New York City.

People celebrate World Laughter Day on the first Sunday of May every year. The first celebration was in Mumbai, India, in 1998. It was arranged by Dr. Madan Kataria, founder of the Laughter Yoga movement.

Laughter Yoga

BEFORE VIEWING

PRIOR KNOWLEDGE **A** In Lesson A, you discussed things you do for fun. Check (✓) the activities you think are fun. Discuss the reasons for your answers with a partner.

☐ a party   ☐ exercise   ☐ a funny movie   ☐ other _____

MEANING FROM CONTEXT **B** The <u>underlined</u> words are in the video. Use the context or a dictionary to help you understand them.

Laughter

Laughter is something we all enjoy. It's <u>instinctive</u>. If we are happy or something is funny, we laugh naturally. And it's <u>contagious</u>—if one person laughs, usually the people nearby will start laughing, too. But laughter is not only fun, it also helps us. It can <u>ease</u> an awkward or difficult situation. It can help prevent certain diseases. It's a <u>behavior</u> that brings people together. We don't know all the ways that laughter works to make us feel better, but the <u>bottom line</u> is that laughter is very good for us.

C With a partner, take turns asking and answering the questions about laughter. Use the information from exercise B and your own ideas.

1. What happens when someone starts laughing?
2. How does laughter help us?

WHILE VIEWING

D ▶ 1.4 Read the questions. Then write the answers while you watch the video.

UNDERSTANDING MAIN IDEAS

1. What do people do in laughter yoga? _____
2. What health issues can laughter help with? _____
3. How many calories can you burn up if you laugh for 5-10 minutes? _____
4. When do babies first begin to laugh? _____
5. How do babies use laughter? _____

E ▶ 1.4 Read the statements. Then watch the video again and choose T for *True* or F for *False*.

UNDERSTANDING DETAILS

1. People tell jokes in laughter yoga.	T	F
2. Laughter has effects that are similar to jogging.	T	F
3. Laughter is present at birth.	T	F
4. Scientists don't know everything about laughter yet.	T	F

AFTER VIEWING

F Discuss the questions below in a group.

1. What was the main purpose of the video?
   a. to tell us about the benefits of laughter
   b. to tell us different ways to make people laugh
   c. to tell us about different kinds of yoga
2. What surprised you about the video? Explain.
3. What are some things that make you laugh?
4. Are you interested in trying laughter yoga? Why or why not?
5. In Lesson B, you will learn about how people use their free time to have fun and be happy. Do you think that people in different cultures have different ways of having fun? Explain.

B Vocabulary

MEANING FROM CONTEXT **A** 🎧 **1.23** Read and listen to what four people say about their free time. Notice each word in **blue** and think about its meaning.

Free Time

1. As a police officer, I deal with **crime** all day long. I like to cook to take my mind off my work. It's a pretty **common** hobby, so I know a lot of other people who like to cook, too. Sometimes, my friends come over and we cook together. We laugh and tell stories.

2. I don't have much **free time** because I have a full-time job and I have children. I like to spend time with my kids when I can. Sometimes we go to the beach, and sometimes we go to the park. For me, playing with my children has some important **benefits**: It brings me happiness and makes me feel young and **healthy**.

3. I **enjoy** taking walks in the park. I love being **outdoors**—seeing the trees and feeling the sun on my face. Basically, I'm always moving. Walking is good **exercise**. All that exercise keeps me fit.

4. When I want to **relax**, I listen to music at home. My favorite music is classical, especially Mozart. There's only one **disadvantage** to spending my free time at home: I almost never spend time outside.

B Match each word in **blue** from exercise A with its definition.

1. _____ free time		a. (n) physical activity that keeps you fit
2. _____ benefits		b. (adv) in the open air; outside a building
3. _____ enjoy		c. (adj) strong and well; not sick
4. _____ outdoors		d. (n) a period when you are not working
5. _____ healthy		e. (v) to get pleasure or satisfaction from something
6. _____ common		f. (v) to spend time doing something calm and peaceful
7. _____ crime		g. (n) advantages; good results of doing something
8. _____ exercise		h. (n) a negative point; something that can create a problem
9. _____ relax		i. (n) an action that is against the law
10. _____ disadvantage		j. (adj) usual; happening often

C Read the article. Fill in each blank with a word in **blue** from exercise A.

An Urban Escape

In a big city such as Paris, people need places to live, shop, and work. Empty space can be hard to find, but it's very important. People need places to spend their _____, and parks are places that most people _____.
     1   2

The city of Paris spends a lot of money to create parks and gardens. Some people think that the high cost is a big _____. So why does the city do this? What are some of the _____ of parks and other green spaces?
     3   4

Better Health. Having places to _____ after work helps people feel good. Parks allow people to get _____, such as walking and jogging. Being _____ in the sunlight is good for people.
  5   6   7

Better Environment. Trees help to clean the air and make cities cooler. Clean air helps people stay _____.
  8

Less Crime. _____, such as robbery and murder, can be _____ in big cities. But research shows there is less crime in places with green areas around them.
  9   10

Improved Education. Parks are also a great place for children to learn and play. According to one study, children learn better after they play in a park.

D Discuss the questions below with a partner.

1. Why do people enjoy parks?
2. What are some disadvantages of spending money on parks?

Somali school girls play soccer during their lunch break.

Listening A Talk about City Parks

BEFORE LISTENING

CRITICAL THINKING:
PREDICTING

A You are going to listen to a guest speaker talk about city parks. Look at the photo. What do you think the speaker will say about the importance of parks in cities?

**Central Park,
New York City, U.S.A.**

> ### NOTE-TAKING SKILL Using a Split Page to Take Notes
>
> One way to organize your notes is to draw a line 2 to 3 inches from the left side of the page. On the right side, take notes on main ideas and important details as you listen. When you review your notes after class, use the left side to write questions that the notes answer. The questions will help you focus on the important points. Writing questions will help to clarify and connect ideas. It will also help you remember information and predict test questions.
>
> What kind of exercise is most important? | Parks good for exercise: walking

WHILE LISTENING

LISTENING FOR
MAIN IDEAS

B 🎧 **1.24** Read the statements. Then listen and complete each statement with the information you hear.

1. The speaker is there to talk about some of the _____ of city parks.

2. The speaker says that parks provide _____ benefits, social benefits, and environmental benefits.

3. The speaker says that _____ is lower in places with a lot of trees and green spaces.

4. The speaker says that healthier, happier people have fewer _____.

C ⌢ 1.24 Read the statements and answer choices. Then listen again and choose the correct answer.

LISTENING FOR DETAILS

1. The first question a student asks is about _____.
   a. the things families do together at parks
   b. the types of exercise people do at parks
   c. the number of people who go to parks

2. The second question a student asks is about _____.
   a. the health benefits of parks
   b. the educational benefits of parks
   c. the environmental benefits of parks

3. The third question a student asks is about _____.
   a. the types of city parks
   b. the drawbacks of city parks
   c. the importance of city parks

4. The fourth question a student asks is about _____.
   a. the health benefits of city parks
   b. the social benefits of city parks
   c. the environmental benefits of parks

D Review the notes from the talk below. What was the speaker talking about? Write your own questions on the left for the details on the right.

NOTE TAKING

Questions	Notes
	Less diabetes, high blood pressure, overweight In hospital, get better
	Less crime Study 98 apt buildings, 50% lower
	Cost • buy land • build playgrounds, walkways

AFTER LISTENING

E You learned that city parks have several benefits. Rank the benefits from 1 to 6 in order of importance to you (1 = most important; 6 = least important).

CRITICAL THINKING: RANKING

_____ People have a place to exercise.   _____ Cities are cleaner and cooler.

_____ Cities have less crime.   _____ People have a place to relax.

_____ Children learn better.   _____ Children have a place to play.

F Work with a partner. Compare your answers from exercise E. Discuss the reasons for your decisions.

A: *I think the most important benefit is that cities have less crime.*
B: *Really? I disagree. I think the most important benefit is that parks give children a place to play.*

B Speaking

When we have a conversation, it is polite to show interest in what the other person is saying. It is also polite to ask a follow-up question to find out more information.

A: *I don't like this TV show.*

B: **Oh? Why not?**

A: *My vacation was fabulous. I'm so relaxed now.*

B: **Good for you. Do you have any photos?**

A: *The movie was just awful!*

B: **Oh, that's too bad. Why didn't you like it?**

A: *It was a fascinating lecture.*

B: **Really? Why?**

A Complete each conversation below with an appropriate expression from the box. Use each expression once. Then practice the conversations with a partner. Switch roles and practice them again.

| Good for you! | Really? | How funny! | Oh, that's too bad. | Oh, why not? |

1. A: I really don't like that new TV show.

   B: _____

   A: It isn't funny!

2. A: Oh, I love this weather. It makes me happy.

   B: _____ Most people don't like rain and cold.

3. A: I'm going shopping. I just got my paycheck.

   B: _____ Don't spend it all at once!

4. A: I'm studying to be a chef.

   B: _____ That's exactly what I want to do.

5. A: I didn't pass the test.

   B: _____ Better luck next time.

B Work with your partner and have a conversation. Follow the steps below. Then switch roles and repeat.
1. Student A: Ask Student B what makes him or her laugh.
2. Student B: Answer the question, and if possible, give specific examples.
3. Student A: Show interest and ask questions to find out more.

C 🎧 **1.25**   Read and listen to the conversation. Underline examples of small talk.

Children playing in a fountain in a city park

Shelli: There are a lot of people here today.

Omar: I'm sorry?

Shelli: I said there are a lot of people at the park today.

Omar: There sure are. It's a beautiful day to be outdoors.

Shelli: It really is. Do you know if it's going to last?

Omar: I don't know, but it feels perfect today. I'm here with my daughter.

Shelli: Oh, which one is your daughter?

Omar: That's her over there.

Shelli: Really? She's playing with my son!

Omar: That's your son? What's his name?

Shelli: Robert, and my name is Shelli.

Omar: Nice to meet you, Shelli. I'm Omar, and my daughter is Zara.

Shelli: It's great that the kids can play here.

Omar: It really is.

D   Compare your answers from exercise C with a partner's. Then practice the conversation. Switch roles and practice it again.

FINAL TASK Presenting on a Celebration or Holiday

> You are going to give a short presentation about something that makes you feel good, such as a celebration, a holiday, or an activity you like to do in your free time.

BRAINSTORMING **A** Write some ideas for your presentation topic in your notebook.

ORGANIZING IDEAS **B** Choose one of your ideas from exercise A. In your notebook, write short notes to help you plan your presentation. Use the example below to help you.

Topic:	Chuseok in Korea
Introduction:	important holiday in fall, families get together
Details:	eat special foods (songpyeon or rice cakes), remember ancestors
Conclusion:	Chuseok celebrates family

PRESENTATION SKILL Speaking to a Group

When you are speaking to a group, you need to speak so that everyone can hear you. Try to speak loudly, slowly, clearly, and with good pronunciation. This will help your audience understand what you are saying.

PRESENTING **C** Form a small group. Follow the steps below.

1. Decide who will present first, second, and so on.
2. While one person presents, the audience listens carefully.
3. After the presenter finishes, each person in the audience must ask one question—either a *yes/no* question or a *wh-* question.
4. The presenter answers each question.
5. Repeat steps 2–4 for each member of the group.

REFLECTION

1. What ways did you learn to show interest in a conversation?

_____

_____

2. What research discussed in the unit surprised or interested you the most?

_____

_____

3. Here are the vocabulary words from the unit. Check (✓) the ones you can use.

☐ amusing	☐ exercise	☐ outdoors
☐ benefit AWL	☐ free time	☐ record
☐ comedy	☐ happiness	☐ relax AWL
☐ common	☐ healthy	☐ researcher AWL
☐ crime	☐ joke	☐ situation
☐ disadvantage	☐ laughter	☐ sound
☐ enjoy	☐ lead	

THE MARKETING MACHINE 3

Pedestrians in Guangzhou,
China, look at a luxury car in a
fish tank.

ACADEMIC SKILLS

LISTENING	Listening for Examples
	Using Abbreviations
SPEAKING	Clarifying
	The Simple Past -ed Endings
CRITICAL THINKING	Applying Information

THINK AND DISCUSS

1 Look at the photo and read the caption. What is the purpose of this image?
2 Do you think this is a good way to sell or market a car?
3 Look at the title. What do you think this unit will be about?

Look at the photo and read the caption and the information. Then discuss the questions.

1. What are some examples of on-demand companies? Which ones have you used?

2. Which industry is the largest? Which ones are just starting out?

3. Why do you think on-demand companies are so popular today?

A row of bicycles for on-demand rental in San Francisco, CA, U.S.A.

THE ON-DEMAND ECONOMY

An On-Demand Company (ODC) provides services such as rides, rooms, and grocery delivery. The On-Demand Economy is the network of companies offering these quick and convenient services.

Key: Industry type

- Shipping
- Subscription
- Delivery
- Pet Care
- Family Care
- Health & Beauty
- Home Services
- Education
- Business Services
- Reservations and Ticketing
- Parking
- Travel
- Transportation

The On-Demand Economy System

Growth by Industry

	INDUSTRIES WITH HIGHEST GROWTH	INDUSTRIES GROWING	INDUSTRIES WITH POTENTIAL	INDUSTRIES JUST STARTING OUT
56% companies founded after 2011	Delivery	Home Services	Shipping	Subscription
	Transportation	Travel	Health & Beauty	Pet Care
		Education	Business Services	Family Care
		Reservations & Ticketing	Parking	

A Vocabulary

A 🎧 1.26 Read and listen to the article. Notice each word in **blue** and think about its meaning.

> ### What's for Breakfast?
>
> A **popular** breakfast food in the United States is cereal. You can find different types of cereal in any supermarket. It's usually in the middle **section** of the store. Cereal boxes are easy to find—they often use colorful **characters** like tigers to **advertise** the **product**. The characters are easy for **customers** to **recognize**, especially young customers ("Look, there's Tony the Tiger").
>
> Many cereals for children have the same **quality**—they are very sweet. Some people worry that companies **aim** too much of their advertising at children, especially when the products aren't very healthy. These people feel we should **encourage** good eating habits.

B Write each word in **blue** from exercise A next to its definition.

1. _____encourage_____ (v) to give support to or help to develop

2. _____ (n) something that is typical of someone or something's character or personality

3. _____ (n) people or businesses that buy from other people or businesses

4. _____ (n) anything that is produced or made with materials and labor

5. _____ (v) to direct something at someone

6. _____ (n) animals or people used in advertising or in a book or movie

7. _____ (n) a piece or part of

8. _____ (adj) well-liked

9. _____ (v) to promote, or make a product or service known

10. _____ (v) to remember someone or something when you see it

---

VOCABULARY SKILL Common Verb Suffixes

Common verb suffixes include: *-ate, -ize/-ise/-yze, -ify,* and *-en*. When you see or hear a word with one of these endings, you know it is a verb.

Suffix	Verb
-ate	*associate, participate*
-ize/-ise/-yze	*analyze, emphasize*
-ify	*identify, quantify*
-en	*harden, strengthen*

C Look at the nouns and adjectives below. Write the verb form of each. Use a dictionary to check your answers.

1. advertisement _____
2. recognition _____
3. situation _____
4. education _____

5. soft _____
6. communication _____
7. creative _____
8. organization _____

D Complete each sentence with a word in **blue** from exercise A. Then practice the exchanges with a partner.

1. A: What kind of food is ___popular___ for breakfast in Japan?

   B: Rice and soup.

2. A: These characters are so cute and colorful!

   B: Yes, I think the company must _____ its advertising at children.

3. A: How is the new store doing?

   B: Great! They had over a thousand _____ on the first day.

4. A: Where can I find the milk?

   B: It's in the dairy _____ .

E Discuss the questions below in a group.   PERSONALIZING

1. Do you buy any products online? Why or why not?
2. What are some ways companies advertise their products?
3. How do ads encourage people to buy?
4. What are some companies or products that are easy to recognize?

A girl makes a mess in a grocery store.

Listening A Newscast about Marketing

BEFORE LISTENING

A Look at the image and read the caption. Then discuss the questions with a partner.

1. Do you know the company or product that uses this character in its advertising? If so, do you like it?
2. How do you think characters like this one, called mascots, help sell products?

Hello Kitty was introduced in 1974. Since then she has appeared on thousands of products.

WHILE LISTENING

> **NOTE-TAKING SKILL** Using Abbreviations
>
> Here are three ways to abbreviate words that you hear:
>
> 1. Write only some of the letters within words, usually the consonants:
>
>   *remember → rmbr*
>
> 2. Use common abbreviations:
>
>   *identify/identification → ID*
>
> 3. Use the first few letters of a word:
>
>   *product → prod.*
>
> Speaker's words: *Companies use mascots to help customers identify, remember, and understand their products.*
>
> Notes: *Comp. use masc. → ID, rmbr, undrstnd prod.*

B 🎧 1.27 ▶ 1.5 Listen to the newscast. Complete the main ideas using abbreviations.

1. Companies use mascots → <u>ID, rmbr, undrstnd prod.</u>

2. Mascots are better than actors because _____

3. Mascots are successful on social media because _____

4. In addition to selling products, mascots can help _____

LISTENING SKILL Listening for Examples

Speakers often use certain words or phrases before giving examples. Listen for these words or phrases, and be sure to take notes when you hear them. The information after them will help you understand the speaker's main points.

For example, . . .	*For instance, . . .*	*Take . . . for example.*
. . . such as . . .	*. . . like . . .*	*Think about . . .*

C 🎧 1.27 Listen again and match each example to the idea it supports.

1. Identify, remember, and understand _____   a. cookie company mascots

2. Name recognition improved _____   b. M&M candies

3. Sharing on social media _____   c. Smokey the Bear

4. Increased sales _____   d. AFLAC duck

5. Helping the environment _____   e. Energizer Bunny

D 🎧 1.27 Read the statements. Then listen again and choose T for *True* or F for *False*. Correct the false statements.

1. One problem with mascots is that they are expensive.	T	F
2. A company may change its mascot to reach new customers.	T	F
3. The name recognition of AFLAC is similar to other insurance companies.	T	F
4. The mascot for Michelin looks like the tires he sells.	T	F
5. *Point of sale* is the place where the customer actually decides to buy the product.	T	F

AFTER LISTENING

E Discuss the questions below with a partner.

1. The newscast presented ways a mascot might be better than a spokesperson. In what ways might a spokesperson be better than a mascot?
2. What mascots do you know? Do you think they help sell products? Why or why not?
3. Think of some famous spokespeople. Do you think they help sell products? Have any of them done things that could actually hurt sales?
4. Think about a kind of product (e.g., running shoes, an electric car, a smart phone, yogurt). What kind of mascot could help sell the product?

A Speaking

Here are some expressions you can use to give clarification when speaking.

No, I said . . .   *In other words . . .*
Let me explain.   *Let me put it another way . . .*
Yes, I mean . . .   *Not exactly.*

Maya: *So, are you saying a mascot is a kind of spokesperson?*
Mike: **No, let me explain** . . .

A Read the conversations. Underline the expressions the speakers use to clarify. Then practice the conversations with a partner.

A: One way we can increase our sales is by using a mascot, like the Energizer Bunny.

B: Are you saying we should use a bunny?

A: No, I mean that we should use something that works as well, but not the same mascot.

A: One thing advertisers think about in their ads is color. Certain colors make us think about certain qualities.

B: What do you mean?

A: In other words, green might make us think about nature and the outdoors, and silver about something expensive.

A: In a few years, cars will be very different. Driverless technology will be in all cars, and people will be able to do something else while riding to work.

B: I'm afraid I don't understand. Will cars drive themselves?

A: Yes, that's what I'm saying. Not all the time maybe, but computers will do much of the driving.

▶ **Coca-Cola Life is the company's first lower-calorie cola that is naturally sweetened. The reason for the green label is to make the product seem more natural.**

B Complete the conversation below with expressions for clarifying. Then practice the conversation with a partner.

A: I'm doing a presentation on logos in class tomorrow.

B: I'm not sure I know what those are.

A: _____1_____ . A logo is a design symbol of a business, organization, or product.

B: Do you mean it's like a sign?

A: _____2_____ that it's like a sign, but a simple one, usually without words. And it's easy to recognize.

B: Can you explain a little more?

A: Sure. In _____3_____ , a logo is a mark or shape that you can use to help customers recognize you or your product. An example is the swoosh for Nike.

C Match each question to the correct response.

1. Are you saying a mascot is as good as a spokesperson?

2. I'm afraid I don't understand. Is a spokesperson a colorful character?

3. What do you mean when you say commercials are one kind of ad?

4. Are you saying that social media can help sell products?

a. No, I said a mascot is a colorful character. A spokesperson is often an actor.

b. Not exactly. A mascot is actually better than a spokesperson in several ways.

c. Let me explain. A commercial is an ad on TV or radio, with audio and/or video.

d. Yes, I mean that if something is widely shared, that's a form of advertising.

D Work with a partner. Discuss the topics below. Take turns explaining, asking for clarification, and giving clarification.

- a mascot
- a spokesperson
- a commercial
- social media

E Work with a group. Review the information you learned in this unit and in other units. Take turns explaining, asking for clarification, and giving clarification.

A: *A hundred years ago, there were a lot more butlers.*
B: *Are you saying that they were popular everywhere?*
A: *No, I mean . . .*

GRAMMAR FOR SPEAKING The Simple Past

We use the simple past to talk about completed actions in the past.

> He **worked** at an advertising agency last summer.
> I **chose** the product with the best reviews.

We add *-ed* to the base form of a regular verb to form the simple past.

We add *-d* if the verb ends in *-e.*

> attract – attract**ed**   advertise – advertise**d**

Many verbs are irregular in the simple past. Some common ones are:

> be – was/were   do – did   have – had   go – went   take – took

Yes/No questions	**Short answers**
Was the mascot popular?	Yes, it **was**./No, it **wasn't**.
Did you **buy** more cereal?	Yes, I **did**./No, I **didn't**.
Did they **go** to the store?	Yes, they **did**./No, they **didn't**.

Wh- questions	**Short answers**
Why was the campaign successful?	Because it was simple.
How did they **choose** that mascot?	It was the cutest.

F Complete each sentence with the simple past of the verb in parentheses.

1. He _____ (sell) advertisements for a local magazine.

2. The company _____ (make) many different products.

3. She _____ (buy) all her holiday gifts online last year.

4. We _____ (find) the cereal in the middle section of the store.

5. That advertiser _____ (aim) its campaign at teenagers last year.

6. The store display _____ (attract) more customers than expected.

G With a partner, take turns asking and answering *yes/no* and *wh-* questions in the simple past. Use the words and phrases below.

A: *Did you eat cereal for breakfast this morning?*
B: *Yes, I did. I ate corn flakes.*

1. you / eat / cereal / breakfast this morning
2. you / watch / television / last weekend
3. what / commercials / be / on television / last night
4. what / you / learn / from the newscast / about mascots
5. how / customers / order / products / before the Internet
6. that company / send / you / marketing information / in the mail

LESSON TASK Discussing a Timeline

A Read the timeline about cereal mascot Tony the Tiger. Then say the sentences to a partner using the simple past.

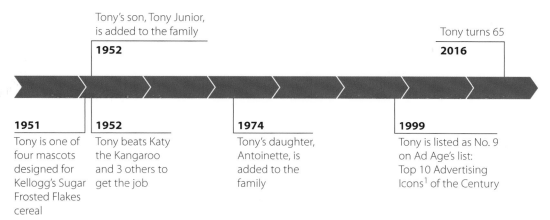

Tony's son, Tony Junior, is added to the family

1952

Tony turns 65

2016

1951
Tony is one of four mascots designed for Kellogg's Sugar Frosted Flakes cereal

1952
Tony beats Katy the Kangaroo and 3 others to get the job

1974
Tony's daughter, Antoinette, is added to the family

1999
Tony is listed as No. 9 on Ad Age's list: Top 10 Advertising Icons[1] of the Century

[1]**icon (n):** a representative symbol of something

B With a partner, ask and answer *wh-* and *yes/no* questions about Tony the Tiger. Use the timeline and your own ideas.

    A: *Why did Tony become the mascot?*
    B: *He became the mascot because he was more popular than the other designs.*

C Look at the Tony that Eugene Kolkey created in 1952 (left) and the Tony of today (right). With a partner, take turns describing the two. Make guesses about the reasons for the changes. Which Tony do you like better? Why?

CRITICAL THINKING: ANALYZING

  > *The original Tony looked more like a cat. The current Tony looks like a superhero.*

Video

The Yuru-Kyara Summit in Hanyu, Saitama, Japan

Mascots: Fun for Everyone!

BEFORE VIEWING

A What do you know about Japan? Take this quiz and check your answers below.

1. Japan is divided into sections called _____.

   a. states   b. provinces   c. prefectures

2. _____ are symbols of these sections.

   a. Mascots   b. Logos   c. Flags

3. The Japanese like _____, a special kind of comic book.

   a. manga   b. miso   c. hibachi

B Match each word or phrase from the video with its meaning. You may use a dictionary.

Word or Phrase	Meaning
1. _____ oversized	a. a chance to take a picture
2. _____ assembly	b. each year
3. _____ licensed characters	c. gathering of a group of people
4. _____ merchandising	d. mascots
5. _____ annually	e. larger than usual
6. _____ PR campaign	f. have a strong effect on someone
7. _____ meeting of the minds	g. agreement, common activity
8. _____ photo op	h. goods made to promote something
9. _____ make a big impression	i. activities to advertise or publicize

Answers: 1. c, 2. a, 3. a

WHILE VIEWING

C ▶ **1.6** Watch the video and choose the correct answer to complete the main idea.

UNDERSTANDING MAIN IDEAS

Mascots are used for _____ .

a. entertainment   b. marketing   c. entertainment and marketing

D ▶ **1.6** Read the sentences and watch the video again. Complete the sentences with information from the video.

UNDERSTANDING DETAILS

1. There are _____ prefectures in Japan.

2. Kumamon is a _____ from Kumamoto. It is a popular mascot.

3. The licensed character industry is worth $_____ a year.

4. This is more than the Japanese spend on _____ annually.

5. Everyone, from children to the _____, likes the characters.

6. The mascots work with the _____, in _____, and on PR campaigns.

7. It is a cute way of _____.

AFTER VIEWING

E Read the sentences below. Choose the best way to end the video.

_____ 1. Because Japan is a beautiful country to visit, tourism is increasing.

_____ 2. Mascots are an excellent way for places in Japan to advertise because everyone likes them.

_____ 3. Characters include Kumamon, who is fluffy, and other characters who are less cute, but who are still fun.

F Work with a partner. Discuss the questions.

CRITICAL THINKING: SYNTHESIZING

1. Did the newscast in Lesson A or the video provide better reasons for using mascots?
2. In the newscast, you learned that companies use mascots to sell products and for public service. How are mascots used in the video? How is this use similar to what was talked about in the newscast?
3. How are the Japanese mascots similar to and different from the mascots discussed in Lesson A?
4. Do you think mascots could be used to promote tourism in any part of the world? Explain.

Vocabulary

A 🎧 **1.28** Listen and check (✓) the words you already know. Use a dictionary to help you with any new words.

☐ achieve (v) ☐ energy (n) ☐ stand out (phr v)

☐ attract (v) ☐ figure out (phr v) ☐ visual (n)

☐ complicated (adj) ☐ join (v)

☐ design (n) ☐ result (n)

MEANING FROM
CONTEXT

B 🎧 **1.29** Read and listen to the information. Notice each word in **blue** and think about its meaning.

Creating a Marketing Message

What **result** are most companies trying to **achieve** with their marketing campaigns? Usually, they want more sales and more customers for their products. First, they need to **figure out** who their ideal customers are. Then they can focus on what will work for that audience.

If you want to advertise a product, you need to think about **design**. What should the ad look like? What kind of **visual** will get people's attention quickly? What will **attract** the most new customers? You also need to think about your message. A simple message is often more successful than a **complicated** one. Your advertising needs to have new **energy** and **stand out** from other campaigns. If it re-uses old ideas and images, it won't get new people to **join** your customer base.

C Write each word in **blue** from exercise B next to its definition.

1. _____ to be easily seen or noticed

2. _____ to reach a goal

3. _____ the power to do work; a quality of being active

4. _____ to solve, discover

5. _____ an effect or outcome

6. _____ the art of deciding how something will look or work using a plan, model, or drawing

7. _____ difficult to understand or explain

8. _____ to associate with, become part of a group

9. _____ to draw in, interest

10. _____ a picture or image used to explain something

D Complete the sentences with the correct word from exercise A.

1. If you want your product to _____ , you need to show how special it is.

2. The park wants to _____ more visitors, so they are hosting some fun events.

3. Rising sea levels are a(n) _____ of climate change.

4. If you want to meet new people, you should _____ a club.

5. My new phone is very _____ . I can't _____ it _____ . I need a simpler one.

6. Luis created an effective _____ to explain his ideas for a new marketing campaign.

7. I'd like to make a table for my office. Do you like this _____ ?

8. If you want to _____ your dream of owning a business, you need to save money. And you're going to need a lot of _____ because you have to work very hard.

E Look at the diagram. Underline the vocabulary words from exercise A. Answer the questions with a partner. Use the information in the diagram and your own ideas.

1. What do you need to know when you are planning a marketing campaign?
2. What or who is an audience?
3. What are different ways or channels you can use to attract your customers?
4. How will you know when you have achieved your goal?

B Listening An Interview with a Graphic Designer

BEFORE LISTENING

> **PRONUNCIATION** The Simple Past -ed Endings
>
> 🎧 1.30 There are three ways to pronounce regular past tense endings. If a verb ends in:
> - a *t* or *d* sound, the *-ed* ending adds a syllable, which sounds like /əd/ or /ɪd/:
>   need – need**ed**   start – start**ed**
> - *f, k, p, s, sh, ch,* or *x,* the *-ed* ending sounds like /t/:
>   look – look**ed**   watch – watch**ed**
> - any other consonant sound or a vowel sound, the *-ed* ending sounds like /d/:
>   play – play**ed**   design – design**ed**

A 🎧 1.31 Listen and check (✓) the sound you hear for each verb in the past.

	/t/ or /d/	/əd/			/t/ or /d/	/əd/
1. graduated	☐	☐		5. worked	☐	☐
2. achieved	☐	☐		6. used	☐	☐
3. wanted	☐	☐		7. created	☐	☐
4. learned	☐	☐		8. posted	☐	☐

B Read the statements about the graphic designer in the interview. Circle the words you think you will hear.

1. She (studied / did not study) graphic design in college.
2. She (got / didn't get) a degree.
3. Her classes (helped / didn't help) her in her work.

WHILE LISTENING

LISTENING FOR
MAIN IDEAS

C 🎧 1.32 Read the questions. Then listen to the interview and choose the correct answer.

1. What is Kate's job?

    a. designing visual art   b. marketing   c. community organizing

2. What is the most important skill she learned in college?

    a. how to think   b. how to use software   c. how to work with clients

3. What kind of ad does she think works best?

    a. one with a lot of details

    b. one that doesn't cost a lot

    c. one with a simple message

D 🎧 1.32 Listen again and complete the sentences.

1. Kate got a degree in _____ .

2. Other companies hire her company to do _____ for them.

3. She's successful if she's achieved _____ the clients wanted.

4. In the example Kate gives, a rowing organization wanted _____ .

5. Kate created a _____ and _____ to attract
   people to the club.

6. Social media is important in marketing because people like to _____
   and companies can get _____ .

AFTER LISTENING

> **CRITICAL THINKING**   Applying Information
>
> When you apply new information, you show not only that you remember and
> understand it, but that you can use it in your own life or in new situations.

E   Work with a partner. Apply what you learned about successful marketing. Complete
the chart about two products or services you both know well.

	Kellogg's Frosted Flakes	Product or Service 1: _____	Product or Service 2: _____
Who is the audience?	children		
What is the message?	"They're grrrreat!"		
What channels do they use?	Cereal boxes, TV ads		
What visuals do they use?	Bright colors, friendly tiger mascot		

Speaking

A Look at the infographic and then answer the questions. Discuss your answers with a partner.

1. Have you seen many infographics? Where? What was their purpose?
2. What features make an infographic good for marketing?

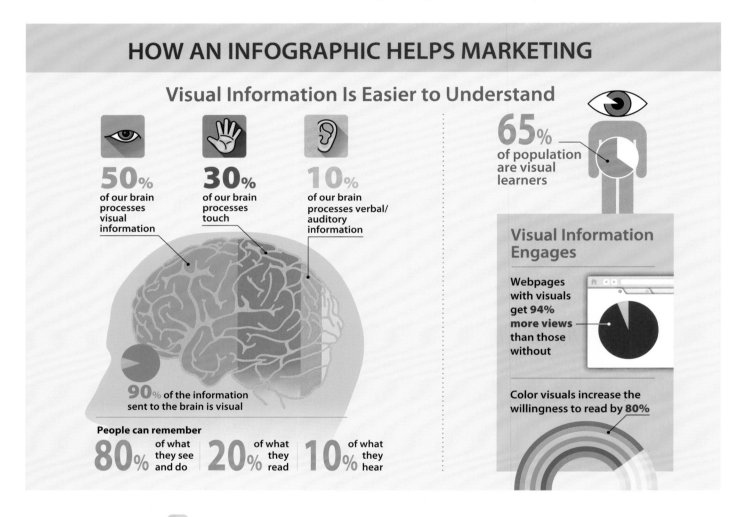

HOW AN INFOGRAPHIC HELPS MARKETING

Visual Information Is Easier to Understand

50% of our brain processes visual information

30% of our brain processes touch

10% of our brain processes verbal/auditory information

90% of the information sent to the brain is visual

People can remember

80% of what they see and do

20% of what they read

10% of what they hear

65% of population are visual learners

Visual Information Engages

Webpages with visuals get 94% more views than those without

Color visuals increase the willingness to read by 80%

CRITICAL THINKING:
INTERPRETING AN
INFOGRAPHIC

B Complete the sentences with information from the infographic.

1. Only _____ percent of our brain processes information we hear.

2. _____ percent of the information sent to the brain is _____.

3. _____ percent of people are not visual learners.

4. People can remember 80% of what they _____.

5. Visuals with _____ are more popular than those without.

C Work with a partner. Take turns asking and answering the questions about the infographic.

1. What are different ways we take in information from the outside world?
2. Why is visual information easier to understand than just text?
3. What kind of information is easiest to remember?

D Discuss the questions below in a group.

PERSONALIZING

1. Do you think you learn more through visual images, doing an activity, or hearing/talking about something? Explain.
2. Do you like infographics? Why or why not?
3. When you look at a website, what do you notice?
4. What kind of information do you like to read on a screen? What do you like to read in print?

E Work in a group. Create an infographic to communicate information about one of the topics in the unit. Follow these steps.

CRITICAL THINKING: APPLYING

1. Choose a topic from this unit (mascots in marketing, mascots in Japanese tourism, or the job of a graphic designer) or your own idea.
2. Make a list of five to seven main points about the topic.
3. Discuss ways to provide the information for each point in a visual way.
4. Create a basic infographic.
5. Present it to another group.

FINAL TASK Presenting a Marketing Plan

> You are going to work with a group to develop a marketing plan for a product or service of your choice. Then you will present your plan to the whole class.

A Work with your group to brainstorm a list of products or services you want to sell.

BRAINSTORMING

B Look at your list of ideas from exercise A. Choose one product or service and write it below. Check (✓) each element you will use in your marketing plan. Then describe it in more detail.

ORGANIZING IDEAS

Marketing plan for: _____	Description
☐ mascot	
☐ message	
☐ TV commercial	
☐ print ads	
☐ infographic	

PRESENTATION SKILL Ending Strong

A strong conclusion reminds your listeners of your main ideas and encourages them to think about your presentation after it is over. To end strong, you can:

- summarize and restate your main points.
  As I said, my product is the best on the market because …
- make a connection between your audience and your ideas.
  This service is ideal for you because …
- suggest an action to your audience.
  Look for my product in your local store!

C Use your chart from exercise B and follow these steps.

- Decide who your customers are.
- Decide what the story or message is for your product or service.
- Create any visuals you will include in your presentation.
- Decide who will present each part of the marketing plan.
- Take notes on what you will say in your part.
- As a group, write a strong conclusion to encourage the audience to buy your product or service.

D Take turns practicing your part of the presentation and making helpful suggestions for improvement to your group members.

PRESENTING **E** Give your presentation to the class. Remember to end strong and tell your audience why they should buy your product.

REFLECTION

1. What skill from the unit do you think you need more practice with?

_____

_____

2. Which part of marketing do you find most interesting? Why?

_____

_____

3. Here are the vocabulary words and phrases from the unit. Check (✔) the ones you can use.

☐ achieve AWL	☐ design AWL	☐ quality
☐ advertise	☐ encourage	☐ recognize
☐ aim	☐ energy AWL	☐ result
☐ attract	☐ figure out	☐ section AWL
☐ character	☐ join	☐ stand out
☐ complicated	☐ popular	☐ visual AWL
☐ customer	☐ product	

WILD WEATHER

4

Extreme snow and cold in
Zhangjiajie, Hunan Province, China

THINK AND DISCUSS

1 Look at the photo and read the caption. When and
where does this weather usually occur?

2 Read the title. What do you think you will learn about in
this unit?

Look at the photo and read the caption and the information. Then discuss the questions.

1. What kind of weather do you see in this photo? How does it make you feel?

2. Have you heard about any of the examples of extreme weather? Do any surprise you? Explain.

3. Look at the details about the extreme weather examples. What type of weather do you think is the most dangerous?

4. What is the most extreme weather where you live?

EXTREME WEATHER AROUND THE WORLD

A storm cloud in Colorado, USA

EXTREME WEATHER

The world is warming, causing an increase in extreme weather. Here are some examples from recent years.

Rain
In the heaviest storm in 60 years, Beijing, China, was flooded with as much as 18 inches (46 cm) of rain in one day in July of 2012.

Droughts
Between 2014 and 2016, Brazil experienced its worst drought in 80 years, causing major water shortages in the city of São Paulo.

Floods
Pakistan had some of the worst floods in its history in 2016, caused by more than 12 inches (30.5 cm) of rain between April 1 and April 4.

Hurricanes
2005 was the most active hurricane season on record in the U.S. with 15 hurricanes. Hurricane Katrina hit New Orleans and other cities, causing severe flooding.

Snowstorms
Winter Storm Jonas was the heaviest snowstorm on record for New York City, USA, since 1869. NYC got 27 inches (70 cm) of snow on January 22–23, 2016.

High temperatures
The temperature reached 123.8 degrees F (51 degrees C) in Phalodi, India, on May 19, 2016.

Tornadoes
The widest tornado ever recorded was in El Reno, Oklahoma, USA, on May 31, 2013. It was 2.6 miles (4.18 km) wide.

Earthquakes
The second-strongest earthquake ever recorded (9.1–9.3) caused a tsunami in the Indian Ocean in 2004 that affected 11 countries. The waves reached as high as 100 feet (30.5 m).

A Vocabulary

MEANING FROM CONTEXT

A 🎧 **1.33** Read the magazine article. Choose the correct word in **blue**. Then listen and check your answers.

Water from the Sky: Too Much or Not Enough?

"How much rain did we get?" It's a question we often hear, and it's an important one because all life on Earth depends on (1) (**storms / rainfall**). As long as our part of the world gets the usual (2) (**forecast / amount**) of rain, we're happy.

The problems come when we get too much rainfall or not enough. In southern China, for example, June of 2016 was a month of (3) (**storms / temperature**) that brought far too much rain. The rain caused (4) (**drought / flooding**) in much of the area. Three hundred people were killed, and 700,000 acres of farmland were underwater.

That same spring, very little rain fell in parts of India. That caused a (5) (**drought / flooding**) in the state of Telangana. The terrible conditions (6) (**destroyed / measured**) food crops, which couldn't grow without water. Drinking water supplies dried up as well. More than a quarter of India's population was affected.

The problems are different when the (7) (**temperature / amount**) is cold. Then it's the amount of *snowfall* that matters. In February of 2016, a huge snowstorm hit the resort island of Jeju in South Korea. It was the biggest snowfall there in several decades.

Because rainfall is so important to us, scientists called *meteorologists* try to (8) (**destroy / predict**) the amount of rainfall different parts of the world will receive. To do this, they (9) (**measure / flood**) air and ocean temperatures. They also watch weather conditions around the world to see how the air is moving.

Meteorologists then make weather (10) (**storms / forecasts**) to let us know how much rain to expect. They're not always exactly right, but they do know when we'll probably have large amounts of rain or not enough.

▶ **Heavy rains in Jiujiang in the Jiangxi province of China flooded a road on June 19, 2016. Rainfall during this 24-hour period reached up to 13 inches (33 cm) in one county.**

B Fill in each blank with a word in **blue** from exercise A. Use each word only once.

1. I remember the _____ of 1987. There was no rain from May through September.

2. Storms with very strong winds can _____ houses. They can be very dangerous.

3. I listened to the weather _____ this morning. The meteorologist said it's going to snow this afternoon.

4. There was a very small _____ of rain yesterday. It wasn't enough to ruin our day at the beach.

5. During the _____, Mike stayed inside the house because he is afraid of lightning.

6. There was a lot of _____ that year—up to 90 inches (229 centimeters) in some parts of the country. It caused a lot of _____, and hundreds of homes and businesses were underwater.

7. The _____ on Friday was 98 degrees Fahrenheit (37 degrees Celsius). It was too hot for me.

8. It's difficult to _____ the weather, so meteorologists are not always correct.

9. Meteorologists use special instruments to _____ changes in the weather.

C Match each word with a statement about the weather.

1. flooding _____
2. forecast _____
3. storm _____
4. drought _____
5. temperature _____

a. It will be sunny on Wednesday.
b. It rained for five days. There was water everywhere!
c. It's cold—only 45 degrees Fahrenheit (7.2 degrees Celsius).
d. I'm not going outside! I'm afraid of lightning.
e. After three years of little rain, it's too dry for plants or animals.

D Take turns asking and answering the questions with a partner.   PERSONALIZING

1. Did you hear or see a weather forecast this morning? If so, what did the forecast predict? Was it correct?
2. Do you usually watch or listen to weather forecasts? Explain.
3. How did you feel about storms as a child?
4. In your opinion, what temperature is too hot? Too cold?
5. What do you remember about the worst storm you've ever experienced?
6. In your opinion, what is "perfect weather"?

A Listening A Podcast about Strange Weather

BEFORE LISTENING

> **CRITICAL THINKING**   Activating Prior Knowledge
>
> *Prior knowledge* means all the things you already know. When you think about a topic or situation, you can use your prior knowledge to help you understand more. Here is an example:
>
> **Topic:** A TV show about dangerous weather
>
> **Ask yourself:** What do I know about this topic? (*Some storms are dangerous. Perhaps they will talk about tornadoes or lightning or typhoons. They might give some advice about staying safe.*)

PRIOR KNOWLEDGE   **A**   You will listen to a podcast about strange weather. Discuss the questions below with a partner.

1. What strange weather do you know about? Why is it strange?
2. Have you ever experienced strange weather? Explain the situation.

B   Form a group with another pair of students. Share your ideas from exercise A. Then discuss the photo on page 67. What do you think is happening? How might it be related to the subject of the podcast?

> **LISTENING SKILL**   Listening for Definitions
>
> Speakers often explain or define terms that are important but may be unfamiliar to their listeners. After an unfamiliar term, listen for forms of *be* in the simple present, or the word *or*, as these are often followed by a definition.
>
> > A water spout **is** a whirling cloud like a tornado that forms over water.
> > Today we're going to talk about weird weather, **or** not your usual rain, sun, and snow.

WHILE LISTENING

LISTENING FOR MAIN IDEAS   **C**   ∩ 1.34 ▶ 1.7   Read the sentences. Then listen and choose the correct word or phrase to complete the main ideas.

1. The podcast is mostly about _____ weather.

   a. ordinary   b. unusual   c. dangerous

2. The definitions of two weather situations in the podcast involve wind whirling, or spinning around very quickly. They are:

   a. waterspouts and   b. fire tornadoes and ball   c. snow rollers and ice
      fire tornadoes   lightning   flowers

3. The speaker wants to _____.

   a. make listeners laugh   b. sell a product   c. inform listeners

D 🎧 **1.34** Listen again. Match the phrases to their definitions.

1. _____ a whirling cloud like a tornado that forms over water
2. _____ a tight whirling cloud of fire
3. _____ a round shape in sky; can be red, orange, or blue
4. _____ an event that can occur when wind moves over loose sticky snow, causing it to move
5. _____ a beautiful crystal formed by very low temperatures and dry air moving over water

a. snow roller
b. water spout
c. ice flower
d. ball lightning
e. fire tornado

AFTER LISTENING

E Discuss the question below in a group.

The meteorologist says, "Ball lightning moves fast and doesn't last long, so it's hard to study." Which of the other weather situations might be hard to study and why?

PRONUNCIATION Reduced *of*

🎧 **1.35** We link and reduce unstressed words in natural speech. The word *of* is reduced to /əv/.

Careful Speech		Reduced *of*
a lot of snow	→ (sounds like)	*a lot-əv snow*
most of my friends	→	*most-əv my friends*
a ball of lightning	→	*a ball-əv lightning*
the rest of the podcast	→	*the rest-əv the podcast*

F Practice saying the sentences below with a partner. Use reduced *of.*

1. I have a couple of questions for you.
2. A lot of people want to know if it will snow.
3. There are droughts in many parts of the world.
4. Suddenly, a strong gust of wind hit them.
5. Most of the storms were still far away.
6. We could get a lot of rain.

A Speaking

GRAMMAR FOR SPEAKING Count and Noncount Nouns

Count nouns are nouns that we can count. They can be singular or plural.

Singular: *a beautiful* **day**, *a* **tree**, *an awful* **storm**, *one* **umbrella**
Plural: *many* **days**, *some* **trees**, *a lot of* **storms**, *two* **umbrellas**

Noncount nouns are nouns that we cannot count. They are almost always singular.

water, **weather**, *bright* **sunshine**, *some* **ice**, *a lot of* **rain**

Some nouns can have both count and noncount meanings.

Count: *He keeps* **chickens** *in his yard.*
Noncount: *He ordered* **chicken** *for dinner.*

	Count Nouns	Noncount Nouns
Affirmative Statements	You should bring **an umbrella**. We need **some tools**. He has **a lot of friends**. She has **three brothers**.	We need **water**. We need **some water**. We have **a lot of time**.
Negative Statements	She doesn't have **an umbrella**. We don't need **any tools**. He doesn't have **a lot of friends**.	We don't need **water**. We don't need **any water**. We don't have **a lot of time**.
Questions	Do we need **any tools**? Do we need **some tools**? Does he have **a lot of friends**?	Do we need **water**? Do we need **any water**? Do we have **some time**? Do we have **a lot of time**?

A Work with a partner. Each of you has a list of words below. Look for information about your words in your dictionary. Then work together to complete the chart that follows.

Student A

cloud	street
flooding	thunder
snow	water

Student B

drought	person
food	sand
lightning	wind

Count	Noncount	Both Count and Noncount
cloud	sand	

A kayaker near Bear Glacier, Alaska, USA

B With your partner, talk about the photo. Use count and noncount nouns.

A: *I see a lot of water.*

B: *Right—that water looks cold!*

C Fill in each blank with *a, an, any, a lot of,* or *some*.

> A: Listen to this: "Climate change is affecting the world's rainfall."
>
> B: Really? Where did you hear that?
>
> A: I read it in _____ magazine article.
>
1
>
> B: I thought there weren't _____ effects on rainfall—only on
>
2
> temperatures.
>
> A: The article lists a lot of effects. _____ of them will happen here.
>
3
>
> B: Which ones?
>
> A: The article says we will probably get _____ very strong storms.
>
4
>
> B: Well, we did have _____ huge hurricane last year.
>
5
>
> A: Right, and remember last summer? We had _____ drought.
>
6
>
> B: True! And didn't we have _____ snow last winter? More than usual?
>
7
>
> A: We did! It was _____ extra cold winter.
>
8

D Compare your answers from exercise C on page 69 with a partner's. Then practice the conversation. Switch roles and practice it again.

E Underline *a, an, any, a lot of*, and *some* in the questions below. Then look at the photo and practice asking and answering the questions with your partner.

1. Does the photo show a drought or some flooding?
2. Are there a lot of plants growing here?
3. What might be some problems caused by this situation?
4. Are any places in the world having a drought or a flood right now? If so, where?
5. Are there some places that are having other extreme weather? If so, where and what kind of weather?
6. Do you see any animals in the photo?
7. Do any people live here?
8. Does this location get a lot of sunshine?

A dry lake in Istanbul, Turkey

LESSON TASK Discussing Travel Plans

Form a small group. Follow the steps below.

Step 1: Imagine that you are going to take a three-day vacation together. Read the list of possible vacation activities. Ask yourselves, *What else do I like to do on a vacation?* Then add three or more new ideas to the list.

- *go hiking in the mountains*
- *have a picnic at the beach*
- *go shopping*
- _____

- *visit some museums*
- *go on a boat tour*
- _____
- _____

Step 2: Read the three-day weather forecast.

Friday

A lot of sunshine today; cooler temperatures in the morning; hot by early afternoon

Saturday

Morning rain showers; thunderstorms possible in the afternoon; clear and cool at night

Sunday

Partly cloudy and warmer; windy in the afternoon, with gusts up to 30 mph (48 kph)

Step 3: Look back at your ideas from Step 1. Discuss your ideas with your group and decide on two activities for each day of your vacation. Then write one morning (a.m.) and one afternoon (p.m.) activity for each day in the itinerary below.

A: *What do you want to do on Saturday morning?*
B: *It's going to rain. Let's do something indoors.*

Friday	Saturday	Sunday
a.m.	a.m.	a.m.
p.m.	p.m.	p.m.

Step 4: With your group, discuss what you will bring on the trip.

A: *I think I need a sweater or a jacket for early mornings and evenings.*
B: *It might be good to have a kite for Sunday afternoon.*

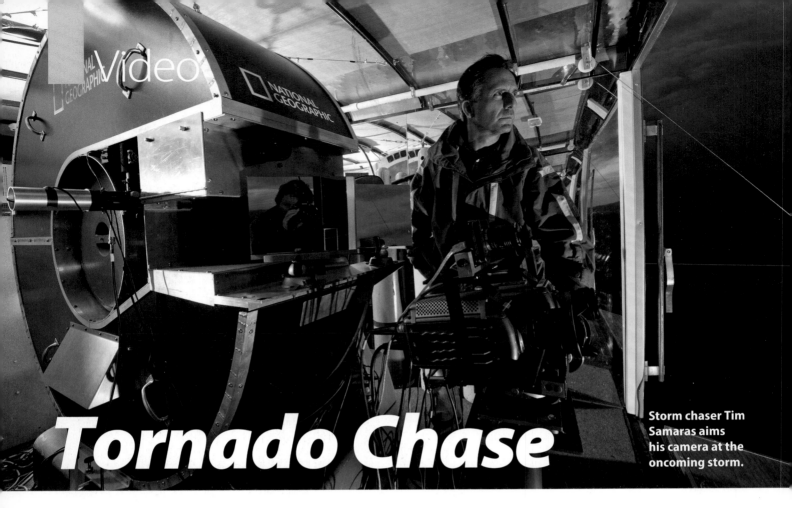

Video

Storm chaser Tim
Samaras aims
his camera at the
oncoming storm.

Tornado Chase

BEFORE VIEWING

MEANING FROM
CONTEXT

A The <u>underlined</u> words are in the video. Use the context or a dictionary to help you understand them.

Tornado Quick Facts

- Tornadoes form during thunderstorms. Their wind speeds can be over 200 mph (320 kph), and they can destroy almost everything in their <u>path</u>.

- Although most of the world's tornadoes happen in North America and northern Europe, tornadoes happen on every continent except Antarctica.

- Meteorologists can't forecast tornadoes accurately. They can only tell people when conditions are right for tornadoes.

- In areas where tornadoes happen, people should have some kind of tornado <u>shelter</u>—a safe place to go during a tornado.

- In order to study tornadoes, some scientists actually <u>chase</u> them! They get as close as possible, and then try to deploy[1] special probes[2] to measure wind speed and other conditions inside the tornado.

[1]**deploy (v):** to put something or someone in position
[2]**probe (n):** a scientific instrument used for collecting information

B Discuss the questions below with a partner.

1. What new information did you learn in exercise A?
2. What do you think would be a good tornado shelter?
3. How do you think people feel when they are close to a tornado?

C Discuss the questions with a partner.

PRIOR KNOWLEDGE

1. How can the weather be dangerous? Make a list; for example, *Very high temperatures can make people sick.*
2. What is the most dangerous kind of weather in your country?

WHILE VIEWING

D ▶ 1.8 Watch the video. Check (✓) the things the tornado chasers do.

UNDERSTANDING MAIN IDEAS

☐ find a road that takes them close to the tornado
☐ go to a store to buy a map
☐ deploy Tim Samaras's probes
☐ go inside a tornado shelter
☐ escape from the tornado

E ▶ 1.8 Watch the video again. Choose the correct answer to complete each sentence.

UNDERSTANDING DETAILS

1. In the video, another word for *tornado* is _____.

   a. cyclone   b. twister   c. thundercloud

2. When a tornado begins to form, the team is _____ miles away.

   a. five   b. six   c. seven

3. The team finds a road that goes _____, directly toward the tornado's path.

   a. east   b. north   c. west

4. Tim Samaras has _____ probes to deploy.

   a. five   b. six   c. seven

AFTER VIEWING

F Discuss the questions below in a group.

CRITICAL THINKING: ANALYZING

1. Why do you think tornado chasers do such dangerous work?
2. Do you think this might be a good career for you? Why or why not?
3. What do you think is the most dangerous kind of weather in the world? Explain.
4. What do you think are some of the most dangerous jobs?

Vocabulary

A 🎧 1.36 Read and listen to the information. Notice each word in **blue** and think about its meaning.

Climate Change

While the *weather* changes from day to day, the word *climate* refers to a common weather **pattern** over a long time. Let's look at how the earth's climate is changing.

Higher Average Temperatures

Although some days are warm and some are cool, the earth's **average** temperature is higher now than in the past. This **heat** means some plants can now **grow** in places that used to be too cold, but the higher temperatures have negative effects as well.

Melting Ice

Much of the world's water is in the form of ice—polar ice at the north and south poles and glaciers in high mountain areas. With higher average temperatures, much of that ice is **melting**. Where there used to be glaciers, we now see bare ground high in the mountains **instead**.

Stronger Storms

The world's oceans are also **slightly** warmer than in the past. This means that the right conditions **exist** for stronger storms, especially hurricanes and typhoons.

Rising Sea Levels

When polar ice and glaciers melt, more water enters the world's oceans and sea levels **rise**. This means that islands and areas of low land along a country's **coast** may soon be underwater.

B Write each word in **blue** from exercise A next to its definition.

1. _____ (n) land near the ocean

2. _____ (v) changing from ice to water

3. _____ (adj) mathematically normal

4. _____ (adv) a little

5. _____ (v) to go up, become higher

6. _____ (n) repeated way in which something happens

7. _____ (n) a high temperature

8. _____ (v) to develop, become larger

9. _____ (adv) in place of

10. _____ (v) to be present

VOCABULARY SKILL Words with Similar Meanings

Many words have similar meanings, but sometimes one is better in a particular context. For example, both *a forecast* and *a prediction* are guesses about future events, but we are much more likely to use *forecast* to talk about the weather.

A: *Is it going to rain later?*

B: *I don't know. I haven't heard a **forecast**.*

Pay attention to how you hear words used, and to example sentences in the dictionary to decide which word is the best choice.

C Choose the best word to complete the sentences.

1. It's going to be a nice weekend. Let's go to the (sea / beach).
2. Much of the ice in the Arctic is (softening / melting).
3. There's been so much rain that the level of water in the lake is (growing / rising).
4. Temperatures can change a lot here in March, but the (average / usual) for the month is about 50 degrees.

D Fill in each blank with a word from the box. You will not use one. You may have to choose between words with similar meanings.

coast	growing	heat	instead	melting	pattern	rising

The whole world is getting warmer, but temperatures in some places are (1) _____ faster than in other places. Greenland is one example. In the past, the weather (2) _____ there was always about the same— cool in the summer and very cold in the winter.

Now, however, the summers are a little longer and a little warmer. People in Greenland aren't buying all their food from other countries. They're (3) _____ more food (4) _____ . Although ice still covers most of Greenland, some of the ice is (5) _____ . That means there is now a little more land, and the land holds the (6) _____ from the sun, so even more ice is disappearing. Greenland's ice won't go away completely anytime soon, but life is changing quickly for Greenland's people.

E Discuss the questions below in a group.

CRITICAL THINKING: APPLYING

1. What information in exercise D is new to you?
2. Look at the map. Where did most people settle in Greenland? Why do you think people still live in those areas?
3. Greenland's ice will probably continue to melt. What effects will this have on Greenland? On the rest of the world?

B Listening A Conversation about Greenland

▶ **Descendants of Inuit hunters harvesting potatoes in Greenland**

BEFORE LISTENING

PRIOR KNOWLEDGE **A** In this section, you will listen to a conversation about the effects of climate change on Greenland. Make a list of things you already know about this topic in your notebook. Use the information on page 75 and your own ideas.

CRITICAL THINKING: PREDICTING **B** Compare your list from exercise A with a partner's. Which topics do you think the speakers will probably talk about?

WHILE LISTENING

LISTENING FOR MAIN IDEAS **C** 🎧 1.37 Listen to the conversation. Then answer the questions.

1. Who are Douglas, Eric, and Lenora? _____

2. Where does Eric live? _____

3. Where do Douglas and Lenora live? _____

4. What are Douglas, Eric, and Lenora doing? _____

> **NOTE-TAKING SKILL** Using a T-Chart
>
> Speakers often talk about good and bad points. Good points are *benefits* or *advantages*, and bad points are *drawbacks* or *disadvantages*. A good way to take notes on benefits and drawbacks is in a T-chart. A T-chart has two columns. On one side, you list the benefits, and on the other side, you list the drawbacks. This helps you compare the two.

D 🎧 1.37 Listen again and complete the T-chart.

Climate Change in Greenland	
Benefits	Drawbacks
shorter winters	

E 🎧 1.37 Listen again. Choose the correct answer to complete each sentence.

1. Average temperatures in Greenland are rising _____ as fast as in other places.

   a. two times   b. three times   c. four times

2. If all of Greenland's ice melts, sea levels will rise _____ feet.

   a. 24   b. 34   c. 44

3. Greenland's minerals are under _____.

   a. land   b. cities   c. ice

AFTER LISTENING

F Discuss the questions below with a partner.

1. Is the climate in your country changing? If so, in what ways?
2. Are you worried about climate change? Explain.
3. What can people do about climate change?

G Form a small group. Role-play the rest of the dinner conversation. Start with the conversation below. Then continue with your own ideas. What will they talk about during dinner? How will they end the night?

Douglas: *Here it is—my delicious chicken with rice!*
Eric: *That looks really good!*
Lenora: *It's one of my favorite dishes.*

EVERYDAY LANGUAGE   Showing Thanks and Appreciation

Thanks a million.   *I appreciate it / your help.*   *Thank you for (doing something).*

Speaking

SPEAKING SKILL Expressing Likes and Dislikes

We can use the following language to say that we like or dislike something:

I (really) like …	I enjoy …	I prefer …	I love …
I (really) don't like …	I don't care for …	I dislike …	I can't stand …

When you say you like or dislike something in a conversation, it's polite to give a reason.

I really like rain because I stay inside and read.

I don't like Greenland. It's too cold for me.

A 🎧 1.38 Read and listen to an interview between a student and a meteorologist.

Student: Do you like being a meteorologist?

Meteorologist: Oh, yes. I really like it. I've always liked science.

Student: Do people get angry with you when your forecast is wrong?

Meteorologist: Yes, sometimes they do, but that's understandable. Even I can't stand it when I want to do something outdoors and it rains!

Student: Did you ever work in a weather station?

Meteorologist: Yes. I worked at a station in Antarctica. I loved it! I did a lot of research.

Student: So you like cold weather then?

Meteorologist: Oh, no. I really don't like the cold! But Antarctica is very interesting.

Student: I'm actually studying to be a meteorologist.

Meteorologist: Really? That's great!

B Practice the interview from exercise A with a partner. Then underline the expressions that tell you what the speakers like and dislike and the reasons they give.

C Take turns telling your partner about weather you like and dislike, and give reasons. Use the ideas and expressions below. Do you have the same likes and dislikes?

A: *I enjoy sunny weather. I can go for a run or play tennis.*
B: *Me, too! I hate snowstorms. Then I'm stuck inside.*

I like …	rainy days
I enjoy …	cloudy days
I love …	thunderstorms
I don't mind …	hot weather
I dislike …	sunny weather
I don't care for …	strong wind
I can't stand …	cold weather
	snowstorms

D Form a small group. Talk about some of your likes and dislikes. Use expressions from exercise C and the topics below. Add at least three new topics.

A: *How do you feel about classical music?*
B: *I love classical music! It's so relaxing.*

science classes	chocolate	sports	cold weather
classical music	fast food	homework	hot weather
Hollywood movies	_____	_____	_____

FINAL TASK Discussing Ways to Reduce Greenhouse Gases

> You are going to explain the process of global warming and participate in a discussion about reducing greenhouse gases.

A 🎧 1.39 With a partner, look up *global warming* and *greenhouse gases*. Discuss their meanings. Then listen to a conversation about global warming. Take notes below on the process and the effects of greenhouse gases.

NOTE TAKING

Greenhouse Gases

_____
_____
_____
_____
_____
_____
_____
_____
_____
_____
_____
_____
_____
_____
_____

B Look at the diagram. Use the words in the diagram, your notes from exercise A, and your own ideas to explain the process of global warming to a partner. Then switch roles.

C With your partner, rank the ways people can reduce greenhouse gases in the air from 1 (most helpful) to 5 (least helpful).

_____ ride a bicycle or take the bus most places

_____ use less electricity at home

_____ plant more trees in cities

_____ buy local products instead of products from other countries

_____ recycle old bottles and cans

PRESENTATION SKILL Making Eye Contact

Whether you are making a formal presentation or just speaking to the class, it is important to make eye contact. Eye contact lets your audience know you are talking to them, and it makes your audience *want* to listen to you.

If you are using notes, look up often and make eye contact. Each time you look up, look into the eyes of a different audience member.

D Form a group with another pair of students. Tell them how you ranked the items in exercise C. Explain your reasons. Practice making eye contact while you speak. As a group, decide on the most important thing people can do to reduce greenhouse gases. Defend your idea to the class.

REFLECTION

1. What skill from this unit will help you the most in everyday life? In school?

_____

_____

2. How has what you learned changed the way you think about weather?

_____

_____

3. Here are the vocabulary words from the unit. Check (✓) the ones you can use.

☐ amount	☐ forecast	☐ predict **AWL**
☐ average	☐ grow	☐ rainfall
☐ coast	☐ heat	☐ rise
☐ destroy	☐ instead	☐ slightly
☐ drought	☐ measure	☐ storm
☐ exist	☐ melt	☐ temperature
☐ flooding	☐ pattern	

FOCUS ON FOOD

5

These women in Mexico City spend all day Saturday preparing tamales for a Sunday meal. Hundreds of people will enjoy the food together.

ACADEMIC SKILLS

LISTENING Listening for Reasons
Using an Outline
SPEAKING Telling a Story with Time Markers
Sentence Stress

THINK AND DISCUSS

1 What does this photo make you think of?
2 Where and with whom do you eat most of your meals?
3 Where is your food grown or made? Is it important to you to know this?

EXPLORE THE THEME

**Look at the photo and read the information.
Then discuss the questions.**

1. What foods do you see in the photo? Which ones do you eat often?
2. Which foods come to New York by truck? Plane? Boat?
3. Are you surprised by any of the information on these pages? Why or why not?
4. What are possible costs to the environment when food travels so far? Explain.

Fruits and vegetables from New York City markets

Fruits and vegetables travel great distances from all over the world to arrive at markets in New York City, U.S.A. On average, the items in this photo traveled 3,371 miles over 4–5 days.

▸ **1 Red grapes**
California, U.S., 2,815 miles
5 days

▸ **2 Red bananas**
Costa Rica, 2,460 miles
7 days

▸ **3 Pineapples**
South Africa, 8,970 miles
12 days

▸ **4 Apricots**
New Zealand, 8,845 miles
1–2 days

▸ **5 Orange peppers**
Netherlands, 3,820 miles
10–14 days

▸ **6 White asparagus**
Peru, 3,645 miles
1–2 days

▸ **7 Chili peppers**
Mexico, 2,685 miles
3–4 days

▸ **8 Mushrooms**
Japan, 6,760 miles
1–2 days

1 mile = 1.6 kilometers

A Vocabulary

A 🎧 2.2 Look at the image. Then read and listen to the information. Notice each word in **blue** and think about its meaning.

THE SENSES WORK TOGETHER TO CREATE FLAVOR

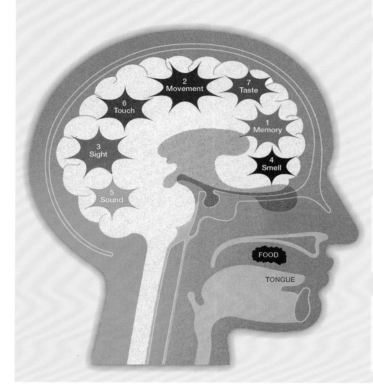

Flavor starts in the **brain**. Our **memory** might tell us we liked a particular food in the past, or we might connect the food with a favorite holiday.

All our **senses** play a role in how we experience food. The movement of food to our mouths, the sight of the food, its **smell**, the sound it makes when we chew—these all feed information to our brain to create the experience of flavor. In addition to flavor, our senses also tell our brain that fresh, brightly colored fruits and vegetables are full of **nutrition**.

People respond to foods in different ways. You might like the **texture** of a soft banana, while I prefer a crunchy apple. The way food feels in our mouths or when we touch it affects how we experience **taste**.

When you see food that is new to you, do you **expect** it to taste good? Or are you **nervous** that you won't like the taste or texture? If we understand why we like the foods we do, maybe we will **waste** less.

B Work with a partner. Discuss these questions about the image.

1. What are the seven senses that together create flavor?
2. Where does flavor originate, or begin?
3. Which sense do you think is most important in how you experience flavor? Give examples.

C Make a list of foods you like to eat. Then discuss the questions with a partner.

_____   _____   _____

_____   _____   _____

1. What memories do you have of the foods on your list?
2. What is your favorite food? Explain why you like it. Use the ideas in exercise A.

D Write each word in **blue** from exercise A next to its definition.

1. _____ (n) body part inside the head that lets you think and feel

2. _____ (n) a flavor; the sense for which the mouth is used

3. _____ (adj) feeling worried or frightened

4. _____ (v) to use carelessly, throw away

5. _____ (n) the ability to remember things; something you remember

6. _____ (n) sight, hearing, smell, touch, and taste

7. _____ (v) to believe that something will happen

8. _____ (n) the process of getting the food necessary for health and growth

9. _____ (n) the way something feels when you touch it

10. _____ (n) a scent or odor; the sense for which the nose is used

---

VOCABULARY SKILL Recognizing Parts of Speech

Some words have different forms when they are different parts of speech. Others have the same form. You can often use the context to identify the part of speech:

*A baby often **responds** negatively to bitter tastes. (verb)*
*A baby's **response** to bitter tastes is often negative. (noun)*
*We **smell** with our noses. (verb)*
*I don't like the **smell** of onions. (noun)*

E Read the following sentences and write the part of speech, N for *Noun* or V for *Verb*, for each underlined word.

1. We underline{wasted} a lot of food when the electricity went out. _____
2. Hearing is one of the five underline{senses}. _____
3. Scientists think sour and bitter underline{tastes} help people to avoid eating foods that might be bad for us. _____
4. My daughter always underline{expects} me to make her lunch. _____
5. Do you underline{smell} something cooking? _____
6. Did you underline{taste} the soup? _____

F Work with a partner. Discuss these questions.   PERSONALIZING

1. Think of a food that you have recently eaten. Describe the senses you experienced as you ate it. Use the image in exercise A as a guide.
2. Do you like to try new foods? Why or why not?

Listening A Radio Show about Ugly Food

BEFORE LISTENING

A You are going to hear a radio show about ugly foods. Look at the photos and the chart below. Work with a partner to add more examples.

Reasons you may not want to eat something	Examples
unusual look	octopus
strange texture	oysters
strong smell	blue cheese
not ripe or too ripe	green tomatoes
your idea: _____	

WHILE LISTENING

B 🎧 2.3 Listen to the radio show. Then answer the questions.

LISTENING FOR
MAIN IDEAS

1. Where are the speakers? _____

2. Why do people like food that looks good? _____

3. What does the nutritionist think about ugly food? _____

> **LISTENING SKILL** Listening for Reasons
>
> Speakers often give reasons to support and explain their ideas. Listening for reasons will help you better understand a speaker's main ideas.
>
> These words introduce or come before a reason:
>
>   *The reason is...*   *... because...*   *That's because...*
>
>   reason
>   *A farmers' market is a great place to shop **because** you can try the fruit.*
>
> These words come after a reason:
>
>   *That's why...*   *..., so*
>
>   reason
>   *Farmers' markets are full of fresh fruit and vegetables, **so** it's easy to find beautiful produce.*

C 🎧 2.3 Read the statements. Then listen again and choose T for *True* if the entire statement is true, or F for *False*. Underline the words that introduce or come after the reasons.

LISTENING FOR
DETAILS

1. Bright colors mean the food is fresh. <u>That's why</u> you should eat only green fruits and vegetables.   T   F

2. You should eat brightly colored vegetables because they are full of good nutrition.   T   F

3. A high sound like a bell can cause something to taste salty. That's because sound can affect flavor.   T   F

4. You shouldn't eat vegetables with a funny shape because they have less nutrition.   T   F

5. Our brains think that beautiful is also good, so we prefer beautiful food.   T   F

6. Fruits have spots and holes because they are unhealthy.   T   F

AFTER LISTENING

D Discuss the questions below in a group.

CRITICAL THINKING:
EVALUATING

1. What foods do you avoid, or try not to eat? Why?
2. Which reason to eat ugly food do you think is the most important? Why?
3. What foods from your culture do people from other parts of the world enjoy? Why do you think they like those foods?
4. What foods from your culture might seem strange to other people? Explain.
5. What can we learn about people from the kind of foods they eat?

A | Speaking

> ### SPEAKING SKILL Telling a Story with Time Markers
>
> When you tell a story, it is important to think about the order of events so that your story is clear to listeners. Notice how this speaker organized her ideas and used time markers.
>
> <u>Tell what your story is about</u>: ***When I was a child***, *my favorite holiday food was homemade cinnamon rolls.*
>
> <u>Give some background</u>: ***During the holidays***, *our family friend always baked a large tray of rolls for our family and delivered them to our house.*
>
> <u>Give interesting details</u>: ***In the morning***, *my mother warmed the rolls up in the oven.* ***Then*** *she put white icing on top of the warm rolls. We children counted the rolls very carefully. We wanted to divide them equally. I loved the rolls because they were soft and warm, and of course, very sweet.*
>
> <u>End your story</u>: ***Even today***, *I can remember the wonderful taste.*

A Think about a food story you can tell. For example, you can talk about:

- a food you eat for a special holiday or celebration
- a memory or event in your life that involves food
- your own idea

ORGANIZING IDEAS **B** Plan your story. Write notes in the chart.

My story topic:	
Background:	
Details:	
Ending:	

Celebrations often involve specific foods. These sweet mooncakes are made from lotus paste, and each has a rich egg yolk in the center. They are enjoyed in many parts of Asia during the Mid-Autumn Festival to celebrate the harvest.

GRAMMAR FOR SPEAKING Descriptive Adjectives

When you talk about food, you want to use details about the smell, texture, color, and taste. Descriptive adjectives help make your ideas more interesting. Notice how they are used.

Adjectives can come before nouns.

> Pizza is a **salty** food.
> **Raw** fish is an **important** ingredient in **Japanese** sushi.

They can also come after the verb *be* and other linking verbs such as *taste, smell,* and *look.*

> This tomato sauce tastes **sweet**.   Peanuts and carrots are **crunchy** foods.
> The fried rice smells **delicious**!   This curry is very **red**. It looks **spicy**.

C Look at the adjectives in the box. Check (✓) those that you know. Work with a partner to find the meanings of any you don't know.

☐ baked	☐ crispy	☐ flavorful	☐ raw	☐ sour
☐ boiled	☐ crunchy	☐ fried	☐ salty	☐ spicy
☐ cooked	☐ delicious	☐ mild	☐ soft	☐ sweet

D Complete each sentence to describe the food (or foods) you will talk about in your story. Use descriptive adjectives when appropriate.

1. _____ is a(n) _____ food.

2. _____ is an important part of _____ .

3. _____ tastes/looks/smells _____ when it is ready to eat.

E 🎧 2.4 Listen to this example. In a small group or in front of the class, take turns telling your food stories. Go back to your plan in exercise B. Use descriptive adjectives from exercise D, and time markers.

> In Nigeria, we eat a special dish with tomato and eggs. When I was little, my mother made it for us every Friday morning. My mother's dish is flavorful and delicious. She uses chili peppers, so it is spicy. My mother learned the recipe from her father, and of course, my mom's recipe is the best!

PRONUNCIATION Sentence Stress

In a sentence, we usually stress content words more than other words. Content words are nouns, verbs, adjectives, and adverbs. They carry important meaning in a sentence. We do not usually stress words such as articles, auxiliary verbs, prepositions, or pronouns.

Listen. Notice that the stressed syllables of the content words are louder and clearer than other words.

2.5 *In Ni**ger**ia, we **eat** a **spe**cial **dish** with to**ma**to and **eggs**.*

*My **mo**ther is a **great cook**.*

*Which **re**cipe is the **best**?*

F **2.6** Mark the syllables of the words you expect to be stressed in these sentences. Then listen and check your answers.

1. When I was a child, my favorite holiday food was homemade cinnamon rolls.

2. In the morning, my mother warmed the rolls up in the oven.

3. Then she put white icing on top of the warm rolls.

4. We children counted the rolls very carefully.

5. We wanted to divide them equally.

6. I loved the rolls because they were soft and warm, and of course, very sweet.

7. Even today, I can remember the wonderful taste.

G With a partner, take turns asking and answering the questions. Make sure you say the stressed syllables of the content words louder and more clearly than the unstressed words.

1. What food did you choose for your story in exercise E? Why did you choose it?

2. What foods do you like to cook? Why?

3. Where do you buy most of your food? Why?

▶ **A family eating together in Dubai, UAE**

LESSON TASK Conducting a Survey about Food

A Follow these steps.

1. Ask a classmate the questions in the chart.
2. Take notes on your classmate's answers.
3. Repeat with two more classmates.

Survey Questions	Name: _____	Name: _____	Name: _____
1. What is one of your favorite foods?			
2. What do you like about this food?			
3. When did you try the food for the first time?			
4. Do you know how to make this food?			

B Form a small group and tell your group members what you learned about your classmates and the foods they enjoy.

> *I talked to Ahmed, and one of his favorite foods is roasted chicken. He doesn't remember when he first tried it, but he likes it because …*

EVERYDAY LANGUAGE   Giving Opinions on Food

More Formal: It's delicious!   Less Formal: It's awesome!
                     It's good.   It's good / alright / OK.
                     It's not my favorite.   It's bad / disgusting! (Yuck!)

C Work with a partner. Practice the expressions for giving opinions on food. Discuss the foods below, and the foods from your surveys. Take turns using more formal and less formal expressions.

| coffee | curry | eggs | ice cream | pasta | pizza | sushi | your idea |

A: *What do you think of pizza?*
B: *It's awesome!*

Tristram Stuart at a farmers' market in Paris, France

Food-Waste Rebel

BEFORE VIEWING

A   What do you know about food waste? Take the quiz then check your answers.

1. How much of the world's food is wasted each year?

    a. one quarter   b. one third   c. one half

2. How much food do we buy and waste each week?

    a. 5%   b. 10–15%   c. 20–30%

3. What has happened to the price of food recently?

    a. It's gotten cheaper.   b. It's gotten more expensive.   c. It hasn't changed.

A: 1. b, 2. c, 3. a

B Match each phrase from the video with its meaning. You may use a dictionary.

Phrase

1. _____ more affluent
2. _____ disposable commodity
3. _____ has no impact
4. _____ blemish or scar
5. _____ how to trigger our evolutionary impulse

Meaning

a. does not affect
b. how to make us want
c. richer
d. a small spot or problem on the surface
e. something you can throw away

C Read the information about Tristram Stuart. With a partner, discuss what you think a "food-waste rebel" is.

> **MEET TRISTRAM STUART** He's a National Geographic Explorer and a "food-waste rebel." The organization he founded, called Feedback, collects food that most people don't want to eat and uses it to cook free meals for up to 5,000 people. The idea is to teach people about the good food that never makes it to our tables. As the world's population continues to grow, throwing away less food could be part of the solution to the problem of feeding everyone.

WHILE VIEWING

D ▶ 1.9 Watch the video. Then discuss the questions below with a partner.

UNDERSTANDING MAIN IDEAS

1. Why do people waste more food now than in the past?
2. In addition to the home, where else is food waste a big problem?

E ▶ 1.9 Watch the video again and fill in the blanks with the information you hear.

UNDERSTANDING DETAILS

1. "Over the _____ years, food has got cheaper, and people have become more affluent."

2. "Big corporations have invested _____ into working out how to trigger that evolutionary impulse to take and take more."

3. "The fruit and vegetables that you buy in the store? It's not _____ for them to look so _____."

AFTER VIEWING

F Discuss these questions with a partner.

CRITICAL THINKING: REFLECTING

1. Do you ever buy fruits and vegetables that don't look perfect? Explain.
2. Stuart says, "Food is land, food is forests…, food is water, food is labor, food is love." What does he mean?
3. At the end of the video, Stuart says we can demand that businesses stop wasting food. What are some ways we can do that?

B Vocabulary

A 🎧 **2.7** Listen and check (✓) the words you already know. Use a dictionary to help you with any new words.

☐ area (n)   ☐ feed (v)   ☐ percent (n)   ☐ solution (n)
☐ crops (n)   ☐ land (n)   ☐ significant (adj)   ☐ survival (n)
☐ environment (n)   ☐ large-scale (adj)

MEANING FROM
CONTEXT

B 🎧 **2.8** Fill in each blank with a word from exercise A. Then listen and check your answers.

Every person on Earth needs food for _____ . Fortunately, farmers

1

all over the world grow _____ such as rice, wheat, fruits, and vegetables.

2

Those foods can _____ both people and animals. There is more than one

3

_____ to the food problem. Back in the 1960s, scientists thought that only

4

_____ farming on huge farms could produce enough food

5

for everyone.

However, the kind of farming scientists believed in during the 1960s required

_____ amounts of water and chemical fertilizers, and also large amounts

6

of _____ to grow all that food on. These days, many people worry

7

about the _____ and the problems caused by large-scale farming.

8

They like to buy their food from small farms instead. In addition, it doesn't take a huge

_____ of land to grow a little of your own food in a vegetable garden. You

9

probably can't grow 100 _____ of your food, but at least you will know

10

exactly where some of your food comes from.

C Match the beginning of each sentence with its ending.

1. There is usually a solution _____
2. I grow flowers and vegetables _____
3. We live in a crowded _____
4. Wheat is a very important _____
5. Most people want to _____
6. My dad feeds his chickens _____

a. area of the city.
b. crop in North America.
c. to every problem.
d. protect the environment.
e. when he gets up in the morning.
f. on a small piece of land behind my house.

D Discuss the questions with a partner.

1. Describe the land in your country. Is it flat or mountainous? Wet or dry?
2. Is farming a significant part of your country's economy? If it is, what kinds of food does your country produce?
3. When you buy food at the market or grocery store, where does most of it come from? (e.g., from your area, from your country, from other countries)
4. Do you and your family grow any of your own food? If yes, what kinds?

During the green revolution of the 1960s in Vietnam, a new kind of rice called "Honda rice" increased farmers' production and paid for motorcycles.

Listening A Lecture about Feeding the World

BEFORE LISTENING

A 🎧 2.9 Read the statements. Then listen to introductory information about Dr. Jonathan Foley from the California Academy of Sciences. Write T for *True* or F for *False*. Correct the false statements.

1. _____ Dr. Foley tries to answer the big questions.

2. _____ Dr. Foley gets quite angry when he talks about these questions.

3. _____ Dr. Foley sees large-scale farming as the solution to our problems.

4. _____ Dr. Foley thinks there are several solutions to our problems.

WHILE LISTENING

LISTENING FOR
MAIN IDEAS

B 🎧 2.10 ▶ 1.10 Listen to the lecture and answer the questions.

1. How much will the population increase by 2050? _____

   How much more food will we need to feed that population? _____

2. Why is the amount of food larger than the population increase? _____

   _____

3. Which three parts of the world could produce more food than they do now?

   _____   _____   _____

▶ **Burning rainforests to grow more food threatens the health of the planet.**

NOTE-TAKING SKILL Using an Outline

One way to organize your notes as you listen is to make an outline. An outline shows the relationship between ideas. A basic outline includes the main ideas and supporting details. You can number the main ideas and indent and use letters for the supporting details.

C 🎧 2.10 Listen to the lecture again and complete the outline.

I. **Introduction:** How to feed the world

II. **Steps**

Step One: Stop deforestation

    a. stop burning _____

    b. grow crops on land size of _____

    c. keep animals on land size of _____

Step Two: Grow more on the farms we _____

Step Three: Use resources more efficiently

    a. example of resource: _____

Step Four: Change how we _____

    a. food to feed people

    b. food to feed _____ and make _____

    c. the fewer animal foods we eat, the more food _____

Step Five: Reduce _____

III. **Conclusion:** Possible solutions

    a. Stop deforestation

    b. Grow more on farms we have

    c. Use resources efficiently

    d. Eat less _____

    e. Waste less _____

AFTER LISTENING

D Work with a partner. Discuss these questions about the lecture.

1. Foley says that how we will feed the world is the most important challenge facing us. Do you agree? Explain.

2. If everyone eats more fruits and vegetables and fewer animal foods, will people be healthier or less healthy, in your opinion? How will this affect the environment?

3. Overall, what do you think about Foley's plan to feed the world?

Speaking

A 🎧 **2.11** Read and listen to two people talk about where they get their food.

WHERE DOES YOUR FOOD COME FROM?

SPEAKER 1

I have always shopped for food at a large supermarket. As a child, I went there with my parents, and now I shop there myself. They seem to have everything I need, and I can get my shopping done quickly. Recently the supermarket added a section with a lot of convenient foods like ready-to-eat salads, side dishes, and even main dishes like chicken and lasagna. To be honest, I don't do a lot of cooking these days!

SPEAKER 2

It might surprise you, but I grow a lot of my food myself. When I was a child, I watched my parents and grandparents work in the garden from spring to fall. I learned to love gardening. Later I discovered that home-grown food tastes much better than food from the supermarket. My favorite things to grow are red, ripe tomatoes and different kinds of lettuce. I also grow cucumbers, onions, and even some strawberries. Everything is fresh! I raise a few chickens, too, and I buy special food for them. That's not all they eat, though, so I never throw much food away. If I cut the top off a carrot, for example, the chickens are happy to eat it!

B With a partner, find and underline the time markers and interesting details in the stories from exercise A. Then tell your partner where you get your food and why. Use interesting details.

Lost and Tossed

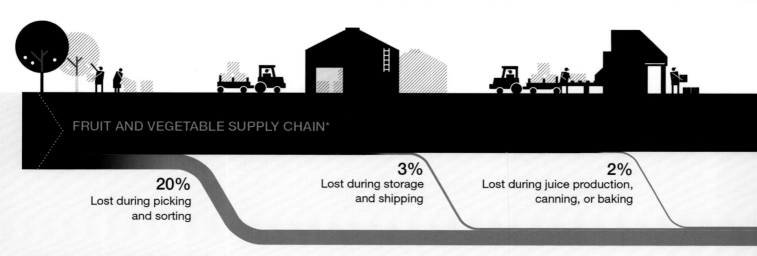

FRUIT AND VEGETABLE SUPPLY CHAIN*

20%
Lost during picking
and sorting

3%
Lost during storage
and shipping

2%
Lost during juice production,
canning, or baking

*AUSTRALIA, CANADA, NEW ZEALAND, AND U.S. DATA ONLY

C Study the infographic at the bottom of the page. Then discuss the questions with your classmates.

1. What does the infographic show?
2. Which countries is this information about?
3. What percentage of fruits and vegetables do people eat in those countries?
4. Which step in the process has the most loss? The most waste?
5. Does this information surprise you? Explain.

FINAL TASK Presenting a Plan to Stop Food Waste

You are going to give a short presentation to a small group about how you can personally prevent food waste. Discuss the information below; then develop a plan to prevent food waste.

A Study the information about wasted fruits and vegetables again. What percentage of food loss or waste occurs at each step or location?

_____ farms   _____ shipping/storage   _____ processing (juicing, baking)

_____ supermarkets   _____ homes

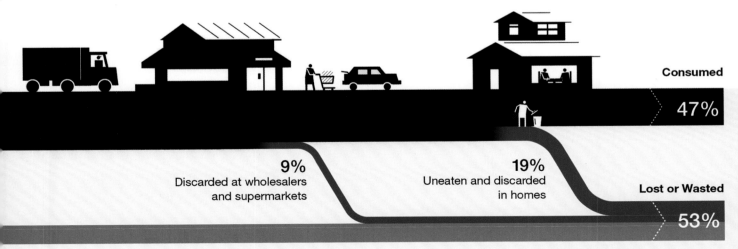

LOST Produce abandoned or discarded during harvesting, shipping, or processing

WASTED Produce discarded by vendors or consumers, often because of damage or expiration dates

Consumed

47%

9%
Discarded at wholesalers and supermarkets

19%
Uneaten and discarded in homes

Lost or Wasted

53%

MANUEL CANALES, NGM STAFF; TONY SCHICK. SOURCE: FAO

CRITICAL THINKING:
EVALUATING

B Work with two or three students. Read the solutions and discuss the questions below.

Solutions for the Problem of Food Waste
- People could buy only the foods they know they will eat in the next few days.
- Farmers could handle and package fruits and vegetables in ways that prevent waste.
- Shippers could ship directly from farmers to markets to reduce storage.
- People could buy locally grown food to reduce the need for long-distance shipping.
- Companies that process food could improve their processes and equipment.
- Supermarkets could accept "imperfect" fruits and vegetables and offer them to customers at a lower price.

1. Based on the percentages in exercise A on page 99, which solutions to food waste would help the most?
2. Which of the solutions can you play a part in?
3. Which of the solutions are out of your control?

PERSONALIZING

C List the two or three best steps you could take to prevent food waste. Consider, for example, the ways you:

shop for food   store food at home   order food at restaurants
bring food to school or work   throw away food   share food with others

PRESENTATION SKILL Using an Effective Hook

An interesting presentation begins with a hook. A hook is something that gets your audience's attention, such as a quote, an interesting fact or example, a rhetorical question, a powerful image, or a short story. Here is an example of a hook that uses a surprising fact related to food waste:

About one third of the planet's food goes to waste every year. That's 2.9 trillion pounds of food that never gets eaten.

PRESENTING

D Present your plan to your group. Be sure to start with an effective hook.

REFLECTION

1. What techniques did you learn in this unit to help tell a story?

_____

_____

2. Based on what you've learned, what changes will you make to the way you shop for food?

_____

_____

3. Here are the vocabulary words from the unit. Check (✓) the ones you can use.

☐ area AWL   ☐ large-scale   ☐ smell
☐ brain   ☐ memory   ☐ solution
☐ crop   ☐ nervous   ☐ survival AWL
☐ environment AWL ☐ nutrition   ☐ taste
☐ expect   ☐ percent AWL   ☐ texture
☐ feed   ☐ sense   ☐ waste
☐ land   ☐ significant AWL

Independent Student Handbook

Table of Contents

LISTENING SKILLS

Predicting

Speakers giving formal talks usually begin by introducing themselves and their topic. Listen carefully to the introduction of the topic so that you can predict what the talk will be about.

Strategies:

- Use visual information including titles on the board or on presentation slides.
- Think about what you already know about the topic.
- Ask yourself questions that you think the speaker might answer.
- Listen for specific phrases that indicate an introduction (e.g., *My topic is…*).

Listening for Main Ideas

It's important to be able to tell the difference between a speaker's main ideas and supporting details. It is more common for teachers to test students' understanding of main ideas than of specific details.

Strategies:

- Listen carefully to the introduction. Speakers often state the main idea in the introduction.
- Listen for rhetorical questions, or questions that the speaker asks, and then answers. Often the answer is the statement of the main idea.
- Notice words and phrases that the speaker repeats. Repetition often signals main ideas.

Listening for Details (Examples)

A speaker often provides examples that support a main idea. A good example can help you understand and remember the main idea better.

Strategies:

- Listen for specific phrases that introduce examples.
- Listen for general statements. Examples often follow general statements.

Listening for Details (Reasons)

Speakers often give reasons or list causes and/or effects to support their ideas.

Strategies:

- Notice nouns that might signal causes/reasons (e.g., *factors, influences, causes, reasons*) or effects/results (e.g., *effects, results, outcomes, consequences*).
- Notice verbs that might signal causes/reasons (e.g., *contribute to, affect, influence, determine, produce, result in*) or effects/results (often these are passive, e.g., *is affected by*).

Understanding the Structure of a Presentation

An organized speaker uses expressions to alert the audience to important information that will follow. Recognizing signal words and phrases will help you understand how a presentation is organized and the relationship between ideas.

Introduction

A good introduction identifies the topic and gives an idea of how the lecture or presentation will be organized. Here are some expressions to introduce a topic:

I'll be talking about . . .   *My topic is . . .*

There are basically two groups . . .   *There are three reasons . . .*

Body

In the body of a lecture, speakers usually expand upon the topic. They often use phrases that signal the order of events or subtopics and their relationship to each other. Here are some expressions to help listeners follow the body of a lecture:

The first/next/final point/reason is . . .   *First/Next/Finally, let's look at . . .*

Another reason is . . .   *However, . . .*

Conclusion

In the conclusion of a lecture, speakers often summarize what they have said. They may also make predictions or suggestions. Sometimes they ask a question in the conclusion to get the audience to think more about the topic. Here are some expressions to give a conclusion:

In conclusion, . . .   *In summary, . . .*

As you can see. . .   *To review, + (restatement of main points)*

Understanding Meaning from Context

When you are not familiar with a word that a speaker says, you can sometimes guess the meaning of the word or fill in the gaps using the context or situation itself.

Strategies:

- Don't panic. You don't always understand every word of what a speaker says in your first language, either.
- Use context clues to fill in the blanks. What did you understand just before or just after the missing part? What did the speaker probably say?
- Listen for words and phrases that signal a definition or explanation (e.g., *What that means is . . .*).

Recognizing a Speaker's Bias

Speakers often have an opinion about the topic they are discussing. It's important for you to know if they are objective or subjective about the topic. Objective speakers do not express an opinion. Subjective speakers have a bias or a strong feeling about the topic.

Strategies:

- Notice words like adjectives, adverbs, and modals that the speaker uses (e.g., *ideal, horribly, should, shouldn't*). These suggest that the speaker has a bias.
- Listen to the speaker's voice. Does he or she sound excited, angry, or bored?
- Notice if the speaker gives more weight or attention to one point of view over another.
- Listen for words that signal opinions (e.g., *I think*…).

NOTE-TAKING SKILLS

Taking notes is a personalized skill. It is important to develop a note-taking system that works for you. However, there are some common strategies to improve your note taking.

Before You Listen

Focus

Try to clear your mind before the speaker begins so you can pay attention. If possible, review previous notes or think about what you already know about the topic.

Predict

If you know the topic of the talk, think about what you might hear.

Listen

Take Notes by Hand

Research suggests that taking notes by hand rather than on a computer is more effective. Taking notes by hand requires you to summarize, rephrase, and synthesize information. This helps you *encode* the information, or put it into a form that you can understand and remember.

Listen for Signal Words and Phrases

Speakers often use signal words and phrases (e.g., *Today we're going to talk about*…) to organize their ideas and show relationships between them. Listening for signal words and phrases can help you decide what information to write in your notes.

Condense (Shorten) Information

- As you listen, focus on the most important ideas. The speaker will usually repeat, define, explain, and/or give examples of these ideas. Take notes on these ideas.

    Speaker: *The Itaipu Dam provides about 20% of the electricity used in Brazil, and about 75% of the electricity used in Paraguay. That electricity goes to millions of homes and businesses, so it's good for the economy of both countries.*

    Notes: Itaipu Dam → electricity: Brazil 20%, Paraguay 75%

- Don't write full sentences. Write only key words (nouns, verbs, adjectives, and adverbs), phrases, or short sentences.

    Full sentence: *Teachers are normally at the top of the list of happiest jobs.*

    Notes: teachers happiest

- Leave out information that is obvious.

  > Full sentence: *Photographer Annie Griffiths is famous for her beautiful photographs. She travels all over the world to take photos.*

  > Notes: A. *Griffiths travels world*

- Write numbers and statistics. (*9 bil; 35%*)
- Use abbreviations (e.g., *ft., min., yr*) and symbols (=, ≠, >, <, %, →)
- Use indenting. Write main ideas on the left side of the paper.
  > *Benefits of eating ugly foods*
  >> *Save $*
  >>> *10-20% on ugly fruits & vegs. at market*
- Write details under key terms to help you remember them.
- Write the definitions of important new words.

After You Listen

- Review your notes soon after the lecture or presentation. Add any details you missed.
- Clarify anything you don't understand in your notes with a classmate or teacher.
- Add or highlight main ideas. Cross out details that aren't important or necessary.
- Rewrite anything that is hard to read or understand. Rewrite your notes in an outline or other graphic organizer to organize the information more clearly.
- Use arrows, boxes, diagrams, or other visual cues to show relationships between ideas.

ORGANIZING INFORMATION

You can use a graphic organizer to take notes while you are listening, or to organize your notes after you listen. Here are some examples of graphic organizers:

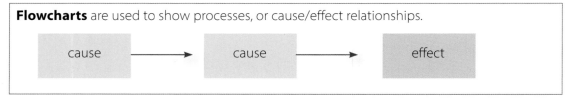

Flowcharts are used to show processes, or cause/effect relationships.

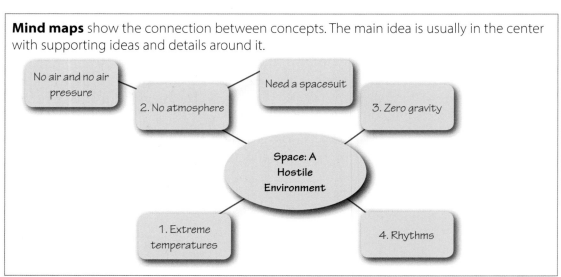

Mind maps show the connection between concepts. The main idea is usually in the center with supporting ideas and details around it.

Outlines show the relationship between main ideas and details.

To use an outline for taking notes, write the main ideas at the left margin of your paper. Below the main ideas, indent and write the supporting ideas and details. You may do this as you listen, or go back and rewrite your notes as an outline later.

> I. **Introduction:** How to feed the world
>
> II. **Steps**
>
>   Step One: Stop deforestation
>
>   a. stop burning rainforests
>
>   b. grow crops on land size of South America

T-charts compare two topics.

Climate Change in Greenland	
Benefits	**Drawbacks**
shorter winters	rising sea levels

Timelines show a sequence of events.

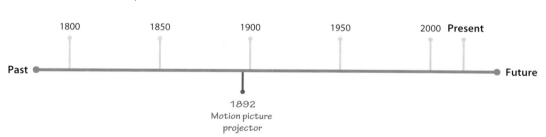

1892
Motion picture
projector

Venn diagrams compare and contrast two or more topics. The overlapping areas show similarities.

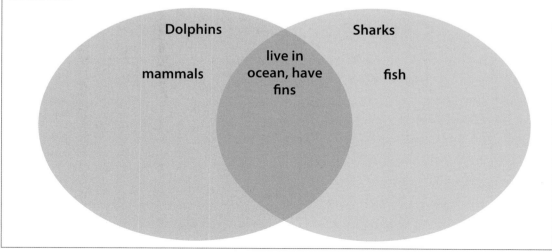

Dolphins   **Sharks**

mammals   live in ocean, have fins   fish

SPEAKING: PHRASES FOR CLASSROOM COMMUNICATION

Phrases for Expressing Yourself	
Expressing Opinions *I think…* *I believe…* *I'm sure…* *In my opinion/view…* *If you ask me,…* *Personally,…* *To me,…*	**Expressing Likes and Dislikes** *I like…* *I prefer…* *I love…* *I can't stand…* *I hate…* *I really don't like…* *I don't care for…*
Giving Facts *There is evidence/proof…* *Experts claim/argue…* *Studies show…* *Researchers found…* *The record shows…*	**Giving Tips or Suggestions** *Imperatives (e.g., Try to get more sleep.)* *You/We should/shouldn't…* *You/We ought to…* *It's (not) a good idea to…* *I suggest (that)…* *Let's…* *How about… + (noun/gerund)* *What about… + (noun/gerund)* *Why don't we/you…* *You/We could…*
Agreeing *I agree.* *True.* *Good point.* *Exactly.* *Absolutely.* *I was just about to say that.* *Definitely.* *Right!*	**Disagreeing** *I disagree.* *I'm not so sure about that.* *I don't know.* *That's a good point, but I don't agree.* *I see what you mean, but I think that…*

Phrases for Interacting with Others

Clarifying/Checking Your Understanding

So are you saying that…?
So what you mean is…?
What do you mean?
How's that?
How so?
I'm not sure I understand/follow.
Do you mean…?
I'm not sure what you mean.

Asking for Clarification/Confirming Understanding

Sorry, I didn't catch that. Could you repeat it?
I'm not sure I understand the question.
I'm not sure I understand what you mean.
Sorry, I'm not following you.
Are you saying that…?
If I understand correctly, you're saying that…
Oh, now I get it. You're talking about…, right?

Checking Others' Understanding

Does that make sense?
Do you understand?
Do you see what I mean?
Is that clear?
Are you following/with me?
Do you have any questions?

Asking for Opinions

What do you think?
We haven't heard from you in a while.
Do you have anything to add?
What are your thoughts?
How do you feel?
What's your opinion?

Taking Turns

Can/May I say something?
Could I add something?
Can I just say…?
May I continue?
Can I finish what I was saying?
Did you finish your thought?
Let me finish.
Let's get back to…

Interrupting Politely

Excuse me.
Pardon me.
Forgive me for interrupting…
I hate to interrupt but…
Can I stop you for a second?

Asking for Repetition

Could you say that again?
I'm sorry?
I didn't catch what you said.
I'm sorry. I missed that. What did you say?
Could you repeat that please?

Showing Interest

I see.	*Good for you.*
Really?	*Seriously?*
Um-hmm.	*No kidding!*
Wow.	*And? (Then what?)*

That's funny / amazing / incredible / awful!

SPEAKING: PHRASES FOR PRESENTING

Introduction

Introducing a Topic

I'm going to talk about…
My topic is…
I'm going to present…
I plan to discuss…
Let's start with…

Today we're going to talk about…
So we're going to show you…
Now/Right/So/Well, (pause), let's look at…
There are three groups/reasons/effects/ factors…
There are four steps in this process.

Body

Listing or Sequencing

First/First of all/The first (noun)/To start/To begin,…
Second/Secondly/The second/Next/Another/ Also/Then/In addition,…
Last/The last/Finally,…
There are many/several/three types/kinds of/ ways…

Signaling Problems/Solutions

One problem/issue/challenge is…
One solution/answer/response is…

Giving Reasons or Causes

Because + (clause): Because the climate is changing…
Because of + (noun phrase): Because of climate change…
Due to + (noun phrase)…
Since + (clause)
The reason that I like hip-hop is…
One reason that people listen to music is…
One factor is + (noun phrase)
The main reason that…

Giving Results or Effects

…so + (clause): so I went to the symphony
Therefore, + (sentence): Therefore, I went to the symphony.
As a result, + (sentence).
Consequently, + (sentence).
…causes + (noun phrase)
…leads to + (noun phrase)
…had an impact/effect on + (noun phrase)
If…then…

Giving Examples

The first example is…
Here's an example of what I mean…
For instance,…
For example,…
Let me give you an example…
…such as…
…like…

Repeating and Rephrasing

What you need to know is…
I'll say this again…
So again, let me repeat…
The most important point is…

Signaling Additional Examples or Ideas	Signaling to Stop Taking Notes
Not only…but,	*You don't need this for the test.*
Besides…	*This information is in your books/on your handout/on the website.*
Not only do…, but also	*You don't have to write all this down.*

Identifying a Side Track	Returning to a Previous Topic
This is off-topic,…	*Getting back to our previous discussion,…*
On a different subject,…	*To return to our earlier topic…*
As an aside, …	*OK, getting back on topic…*
That reminds me…	*So to return to what we were saying,…*

Signaling a Definition	Talking about Visuals
Which means…	*This graph/infographic/diagram shows/explains…*
What that means is…	*The line/box/image represents…*
Or…	*The main point of this visual is…*
In other words,…	*You can see…*
Another way to say that is…	*From this we can see…*
That is…	
That is to say…	

Conclusion

Concluding	
Well/So, that's how I see it.	*To sum up,*
In conclusion,	*As you can see,…*
In summary,	*At the end,…*
	To review, (+ restatement of main points)

PRESENTATION STRATEGIES

You will often have to give individual or group presentations in your class. The strategies below will help you to prepare, present, and reflect on your presentations.

Prepare

As you prepare your presentation:

Consider Your Topic

- **Choose a topic you feel passionate about.** If you are passionate about your topic, your audience will be more interested and excited about your topic, too. Focus on one major idea that you can bring to life. The best ideas are the ones your audience wants to experience.

Consider Your Purpose

- **Have a strong start.** Use an effective hook, such as a quote, an interesting example, a rhetorical question, or a powerful image to get your audience's attention. Include one sentence that explains what you will do in your presentation and why.
- **Stay focused.** Make sure your details and examples support your main points. Avoid sidetracks or unnecessary information that takes you away from your topic.
- **Use visuals that relate to your ideas.** Drawings, photos, video clips, infographics, charts, maps, slides, and physical objects can get your audience's attention and explain ideas effectively. For example, a photo or map of a location you mention can help your audience picture a place they have never been. Slides with only key words and phrases can help emphasize your main points. Visuals should be bright, clear, and simple.
- **Have a strong conclusion.** A strong conclusion should serve the same purpose as a strong start—to get your audience's attention and make them think. Good conclusions often refer back to the introduction, or beginning of the presentation. For example, if you ask a question in the beginning, you can answer it in the conclusion. Remember to restate your main points, and add a conclusion device such as a question, a call to action, or a quote.

Consider your Audience

- **Use familiar concepts.** Think about the people in your audience. Ask yourself these questions: Where are they from? How old are they? What is their background? What do they already know about my topic? What information do I need to explain? Use language and concepts they will understand.
- **Share a personal story.** Consider presenting information that will get an emotional reaction; for example, information that will make your audience feel surprised, curious, worried, or upset. This will help your audience relate to you and your topic.
- **Be authentic (be yourself!).** Write your presentation yourself. Use words that you know and are comfortable using.

Rehearse

- **Make an outline** to help you organize your ideas.
- **Write notes on notecards.** Do not write full sentences, just key words and phrases to help you remember important ideas. Mark the words you should stress and places to pause.
- **Review pronunciation.** Check the pronunciation of words you are uncertain about with a classmate, a teacher, or in a dictionary. Note and practice the pronunciation of difficult words.
- **Memorize the introduction and conclusion.** Rehearse your presentation several times. Practice saying it out loud to yourself (perhaps in front of a mirror or video recorder) and in front of others.
- **Ask for feedback.** Note and revise information that doesn't flow smoothly based on feedback and on your own performance in rehearsal. If specific words or phrases are still a problem, rephrase them.

Present

As you present:

- **Pay attention to your pacing** (how fast or slow you speak). Remember to speak slowly and clearly. Pause to allow your audience to process information.
- **Speak at a volume loud enough to be heard** by everyone in the audience, but not too loud. Ask the audience if your volume is OK at the beginning of your talk.

- **Vary your intonation.** Don't speak in the same tone throughout the talk. Your audience will be more interested if your voice rises and falls, speeds up and slows down to match the ideas you are talking about.
- **Be friendly and relaxed with your audience**—remember to smile!
- **Show enthusiasm for your topic.** Use humor if appropriate.
- **Have a relaxed body posture.** Don't stand with your arms folded, or look down at your notes. Use gestures when helpful to emphasize your points.
- **Don't read directly from your notes.** Use them to help you remember ideas.
- **Don't look at or read from your visuals too much.** Use them to support your ideas.
- **Make frequent eye contact** with the entire audience.

Reflect

As you reflect on your presentation:

- **Consider what you think went well** during your presentation and what areas you can improve upon.
- **Get feedback** from your classmates and teacher. How do their comments relate to your own thoughts about your presentation? Did they notice things you didn't? How can you use their feedback in your next presentation?

PRESENTATION OUTLINE

When you are planning a presentation, you may find it helpful to use an outline. If it is a group presentation, the outline can provide an easy way to divide the content. For example, one student can do the introduction, another student the first idea in the body, and so on.

1. Introduction

    Topic: _____

    Hook: _____

    Statement of main idea: _____

2. Body

    First step/example/reason: _____

      Supporting details: _____ _____ _____

    Second step/example/reason: _____

      Supporting details: _____ _____ _____

    Third step/example/reason: _____

      Supporting details: _____ _____ _____

3. Conclusion

    Main points to summarize: _____ _____

    Suggestions/Predictions: _____ _____

    Closing comments/summary: _____

PRONUNCIATION GUIDE

Sounds and Symbols

Vowels

Symbol	Key Words
/ɑ/	hot, stop
/æ/	cat, ran
/aɪ/	fine, nice
/i/	eat, need
/ɪ/	sit, him
/eɪ/	name, say
/ɛ/	get, bed
/ʌ/	cup, what
/ə/	about, lesson
/u/	boot, new
/ʊ/	book, could
/oʊ/	go, road
/ɔ/	law, walk
/aʊ/	house, now
/ɔɪ/	toy, coin

Consonants

Symbol	Key Word	Symbol	Key Word
/b/	boy	/t/	tea
/d/	day	/tʃ/	cheap
/dʒ/	job, bridge	/v/	vote
/f/	face	/w/	we
/g/	go	/y/	yes
/h/	hat	/z/	zoo
/k/	key, car		
/l/	love	/ð/	they
/m/	my	/θ/	think
/n/	nine	/ʃ/	shoe
/ŋ/	sing	/ʒ/	measure
/p/	pen		
/r/	right		
/s/	see		

Source: *The Newbury House Dictionary plus Grammar Reference*, Fifth Edition, National Geographic Learning/ Cengage Learning, 2014.

Rhythm

The rhythm of English involves stress and pausing.

Stress

• English words are based on syllables—units of sound that include one vowel sound.

• In every word in English, one syllable has the primary stress.

• In English, speakers group words that go together based on the meaning and context of the sentence. These groups of words are called *thought groups*. In each thought group, one word is stressed more than the others—the stress is placed on the syllable with the primary stress in this word.

• In general, new ideas and information are stressed.

Pausing

• Pauses in English can be divided into two groups: long and short pauses.

• English speakers use long pauses to mark the conclusion of a thought, items in a list, or choices given.

• Short pauses are used in between thought groups to break up the ideas in sentences into smaller, more manageable chunks of information.

Intonation

English speakers use intonation, or pitch (the rise and fall of their voice), to help express meaning. For example, speakers usually use a rising intonation at the end of *yes/no* questions, and a falling intonation at the end of *wh-* questions and statements.

VOCABULARY BUILDING STRATEGIES

Vocabulary learning is an on-going process. The strategies below will help you learn and remember new vocabulary words.

Guessing Meaning from Context

You can often guess the meaning of an unfamiliar word by looking at or listening to the words and sentences around it. Speakers usually know when a word is unfamiliar to the audience, or is essential to understanding the main ideas, and often provide clues to its meaning.

- Repetition: A speaker may use the same key word or phrase, or use another form of the same word.
- Restatement or synonym: A speaker may give a synonym to explain the meaning of a word, using phrases such as, *in other words, also called, or…, also known as.*
- Antonyms: A speaker may define a word by explaining what it is NOT. The speaker may say *Unlike A/In contrast to A, B is…*
- Definition: Listen for signals such as *which means* or *is defined as*. Definitions can also be signaled by a pause.
- Examples: A speaker may provide examples that can help you figure out what something is. For example, ***Mascots*** *are a very popular marketing tool. You've seen them on commercials and in ads on social media –* ***cute, brightly colored creatures that help sell a product***.

Understanding Word Families: Stems, Prefixes, and Suffixes

Use your understanding of stems, prefixes, and suffixes to recognize unfamiliar words and to expand your vocabulary. The stem is the root part of the word, which provides the main meaning. A prefix comes before the stem and usually modifies meaning (e.g., adding *re-* to a word means "again" or "back"). A suffix comes after the stem and usually changes the part of speech (e.g., adding *-ion, -tion,* or *-ation* to a verb changes it to a noun). Words that share the same stem or root belong to the same word family (e.g., *event, eventful, uneventful, uneventfully*).

Word Stem	Meaning	Example
ann, enn	year	anniversary, millennium
chron(o)	time	chronological, synchronize
flex, flect	bend	flexible, reflection
graph	draw, write	graphics, paragraph
lab	work	labor, collaborate
mob, mot, mov	move	automobile, motivate, mover
port	carry	transport, import
sect	cut	sector, bisect

Prefix	Meaning	Example
dis-	not, opposite of	disappear, disadvantages
in-, im-, il-, ir-	not	inconsistent, immature, illegal, irresponsible
inter-	between	Internet, international
mis-	bad, badly, incorrectly	misunderstand, misjudge
pre-	before	prehistoric, preheat
re-	again; back	repeat; return
trans-	across, beyond	transfer, translate
un-	not	uncooked, unfair

Suffix	Meaning	Example
-able, -ible	worth, ability	believable, impossible
-en	to cause to become; made of	lengthen, strengthen; golden
-er, -or	one who	teacher, director
-ful	full of	beautiful, successful
-ify, -fy	to make or become	simplify, satisfy
-ion, -tion, -ation	condition, action	occasion, education, foundation
-ize	cause	modernize, summarize
-ly	in the manner of	carefully, happily
-ment	condition or result	assignment, statement
-ness	state of being	happiness, sadness

Using a Dictionary

Here are some tips for using a dictionary:

- When you see or hear a new word, try to guess its part of speech (noun, verb, adjective, etc.) and meaning, then look it up in a dictionary.
- Some words have multiple meanings. Look up a new word in the dictionary and try choose the correct meaning for the context. Then see if it makes sense within the context.
- When you look up a word, look at all the definitions to see if there is a basic core meaning. This will help you understand the word when it is used in a different context. Also look at all the related words, or words in the same family. This can help you expand your vocabulary. For example, the core meaning of *structure* involves something built or put together.

> **structure** /ˈstrʌktʃər/ *n.* **1** [C] a building of any kind: *A new structure is being built on the corner.* **2** [C] any architectural object of any kind: *The Eiffel Tower is a famous Parisian structure.* **3** [U] the way parts are put together or organized: *the structure of a song‖a business's structure*
> –*v.* [T] **-tured, -turing, -tures** to put together or organize parts of s.t.: *We are structuring a plan to hire new teachers.*
> -*adj.* **structural.**

Source: *The Newbury House Dictionary plus Grammar Reference*, Fifth Edition, National Geographic Learning/Cengage Learning, 2014

Multi-Word Units

You can improve your fluency if you learn and use vocabulary as multi-word units: idioms (*go the extra mile*), collocations (*wide range*), and fixed expressions (*in other words*). Some multi-word units can only be understood as a chunk – the individual words do not add up to the same overall meaning. Keep track of multi-word units in a notebook or on notecards.

Vocabulary Note Cards

You can expand your vocabulary by using vocabulary note cards or a vocabulary building app. Write the word, expression, or sentence that you want to learn on one side. On the other, draw a four-square grid and write the following information in the squares: definition; translation (in your first language); sample sentence; synonyms. Choose words that are high frequency or on the academic word list. If you have looked a word up a few times, you should make a card for it.

definition:	first language translation:
sample sentence:	synonyms:

Organize the cards in review sets so you can practice them. Don't put words that are similar in spelling or meaning in the same review set as you may get them mixed up. Go through the cards and test yourself on the words or expressions. You can also practice with a partner.

VOCABULARY INDEX

Word	Page	CEFR† Level	Word	Page	CEFR† Level	Word	Page	CEFR† Level
public	144	B2	rise	74	B1	stand out	54	B2
quality	44	B1	save	174	B1	storm	64	A2
rainfall	64	off list	scenery	174	B1	stressful*	124	B1
raise	164	B2	sculpture	144	B1	support (v)	194	B1
rapid	114	B2	search	14	B1	survival*	94	B2
reach	134	B2	section*	44	B1	taste (n)	84	B1
recent	194	B1	sense (n)	84	B2	technology*	104	B1
recognize / recognise	44	B1	share	164	A2	temperature	64	A2
record (v)	24	B2	sign (n)	194	B1	temporary*	144	B1
reflect	134	B2	significant*	94	B2	texture	84	C1
relationship	164	B1	similar*	174	B1	tourist	114	A2
relax*	34	B1	simple	154	B1	traditional*	154	B1
remove*	104	B1	situation	24	B1	typical	154	B1
repeat (v)	144	A2	size	134	A2	value (v)	164	B2
represent	184	B2	skill	4	B1	view (v)	134	C2
require*	174	B1	slightly	74	B2	visual* (n)	54	B1
researcher*	24	B2	smell (n)	84	B1	waste (v)	84	B1
resident*	104	B2	solid	144	B2	wide	184	A2
respect (n)	164	B1	solution	94	B1	wildlife	174	B1
responsibility	164	B2	sound	24	A2	within	164	B2
result (n)	54	B1	speech	194	B1	zone	104	B1
			speed	184	B1			

†The Common European Framework of Reference for Languages (CEFR) is an international standard for describing language proficiency. *Pathways* Level 1 is intended for students at CEFR levels A2–B1. The target vocabulary is at the following CEFR levels: A1: 1%; A2: 12%; B1: 63%; B2: 20%; C1: 1.5%; C2: 1%; off list: 1.5%.

*These words are on the Academic Word List (AWL). The AWL is a list of the 570 highest-frequency academic word families that regularly appear in academic texts. The AWL was compiled by researcher Averil Coxhead based on her analysis of a 3.5-million-word corpus (Coxhead, 2000).

RUBRICS

UNIT 1   Lesson B Final Task

Check (✓) if the presenter did the following:

	Name		
	_____	_____	_____
1. introduced herself or himself	☐	☐	☐
2. gave information about where she/he is from	☐	☐	☐
3. gave information about what she/he is studying	☐	☐	☐
4. gave information about the job she/he has or hopes to have	☐	☐	☐
5. included reason(s) for choosing this job	☐	☐	☐
OVERALL RATING Note: 1 = lowest; 5 = highest	1 2 3 4 5	1 2 3 4 5	1 2 3 4 5
Notes:			

UNIT 2   Lesson B Final Task

Check (✓) if the presenter did the following:

	Name		
	_____	_____	_____
1. included an introduction, which explained his or her topic	☐	☐	☐
2. included supporting details	☐	☐	☐
3. included a conclusion	☐	☐	☐
4. spoke loudly, slowly, and clearly	☐	☐	☐
5. answered the audience's questions	☐	☐	☐
OVERALL RATING Note: 1 = lowest; 5 = highest	1 2 3 4 5	1 2 3 4 5	1 2 3 4 5
Notes:			

UNIT 3   Lesson B Final Task

Check (✓) if the presenters did the following:

	Name		
	_____	_____	_____
1. presented a clear marketing plan with one or more elements	☐	☐	☐
2. described the product or service well	☐	☐	☐
3. included good visuals	☐	☐	☐
4. included a strong conclusion that summarized the main ideas of the plan and sold the product	☐	☐	☐
OVERALL RATING Note: 1 = lowest; 5 = highest	1 2 3 4 5	1 2 3 4 5	1 2 3 4 5
Notes:			

UNIT 4   Lesson B Final Task

Check (✓) if the presenter did the following:

	Name		
	_____	_____	_____
1. used information from the diagram to explain the process	☐	☐	☐
2. explained reasons for ranking items	☐	☐	☐
3. made eye contact while speaking	☐	☐	☐
4. successfully defended ideas	☐	☐	☐
OVERALL RATING Note: 1 = lowest; 5 = highest	1 2 3 4 5	1 2 3 4 5	1 2 3 4 5
Notes:			

UNIT 5 Lesson B Final Task

Check (✓) if the presenter did the following:

	Name		
	_____	_____	_____
1. started with an effective hook	☐	☐	☐
2. chose good solutions based on the information	☐	☐	☐
3. presented his or her personal plan clearly	☐	☐	☐
4. included two or three steps to prevent food waste	☐	☐	☐
OVERALL RATING Note: 1 = lowest; 5 = highest	1 2 3 4 5	1 2 3 4 5	1 2 3 4 5
Notes:			

ACKNOWLEDGEMENTS

The Authors and Publisher would like to acknowledge the teachers around the world who participated in the development of the second edition of *Pathways*.

A special thanks to our Advisory Board for their valuable input during the development of this series.

ADVISORY BOARD

Mahmoud Al Hosni, Modern College of Business and Science, Muscat; **Safaa Al-Salim**, Kuwait University, Kuwait City; **Laila AlQadhi**, Kuwait University, Kuwait City; **Julie Bird**, RMIT University Vietnam, Ho Chi Minh City; **Elizabeth Bowles**, Virginia Tech Language and Culture Institute, Blacksburg, VA; **Rachel Bricker**, Arizona State University, Tempe, AZ; **James Broadbridge**, J.F. Oberlin University, Tokyo; **Marina Broeder**, Mission College, Santa Clara, CA; **Shawn Campbell**, Hangzhou High School, Hangzhou; **Trevor Carty**, James Cook University, Singapore; **Jindarat De Vleeschauwer**, Chiang Mai University, Chiang Mai; **Wai-Si El Hassan**, Prince Mohammad Bin Fahd University, Dhahran; **Jennifer Farnell**, University of Bridgeport, Bridgeport, CT; **Rasha Gazzaz**, King Abdulaziz University, Jeddah; **Keith Graziadei**, Santa Monica College, Santa Monica, CA; **Janet Harclerode**, Santa Monica Community College, Santa Monica, CA; **Anna Hasper**, TeacherTrain, Dubai; **Phoebe Kamel Yacob Hindi**, Abu Dhabi Vocational Education and Training Institute, Abu Dhabi; **Kuei-ping Hsu**, National Tsing Hua University, Hsinchu; **Greg Jewell**, Drexel University, Philadelphia, PA; **Adisra Katib**, Chulalongkorn University Language Institute, Bangkok; **Wayne Kennedy**, LaGuardia Community College, Long Island City, NY; **Beth Koo**, Central Piedmont Community College, Charlotte, NC; **Denise Kray**, Bridge School, Denver, CO; **Chantal Kruger**, ILA Vietnam, Ho Chi Minh City; **William P. Kyzner**, Fuyang AP Center, Fuyang; **Becky Lawrence**, Massachusetts International Academy, Marlborough, MA; **Deborah McGraw**, Syracuse University, Syracuse, NY; **Mary Moore**, University of Puerto Rico, San Juan; **Raymond Purdy**, ELS Language Centers, Princeton, NJ; **Anouchka Rachelson**, Miami Dade College, Miami, FL; **Fathimah Razman**, Universiti Utara Malaysia, Sintok; **Phil Rice**, University of Delaware ELI, Newark, DE; **Scott Rousseau**, American University of Sharjah, Sharjah; **Verna Santos-Nafrada**, King Saud University, Riyadh; **Eugene Sidwell**, American Intercon Institute, Phnom Penh; **Gemma Thorp**, Monash University English Language Centre, Melbourne; **Matt Thurston**, University of Central Lancashire, Preston; **Christine Tierney**, Houston Community College, Houston, TX; **Jet Robredillo Tonogbanua**, FPT University, Hanoi.

GLOBAL REVIEWERS

ASIA

Antonia Cavcic, Asia University, Tokyo; **Soyhan Egitim**, Tokyo University of Science, Tokyo; **Caroline Handley**, Asia University, Tokyo; **Patrizia Hayashi**, Meikai University, Urayasu; **Greg Holloway**, University of Kitakyushu, Kitakyushu; **Anne C. Ihata**, Musashino University, Tokyo; **Kathryn Mabe**, Asia University, Tokyo; **Frederick Navarro Bacala**, Yokohama City University, Yokohama; **Tyson Rode**, Meikai University, Urayasu; **Scott Shelton-Strong**, Asia University, Tokyo; **Brooks Slaybaugh**, Yokohama City University, Yokohama; **Susanto Sugiharto**, Sutomo Senior High School, Medan; **Andrew Zitzmann**, University of Kitakyushu, Kitakyushu

LATIN AMERICA AND THE CARIBBEAN

Raul Bilini, ProLingua, Dominican Republic; **Alejandro Garcia**, Collegio Marcelina, Mexico; **Humberto Guevara**, Tec de Monterrey, Campus Monterrey, Mexico; **Romina Olga Planas**, Centro Cultural Paraguayo Americano, Paraguay; **Carlos Rico-Troncoso**, Pontificia Universidad Javeriana, Colombia; **Ialê Schetty**, Enjoy English, Brazil; **Aline Simoes**, Way To Go Private English, Brazil; **Paulo Cezar Lira Torres**, APenglish, Brazil; **Rosa Enilda Vasquez**, Swisher Dominicana, Dominican Republic; **Terry Whitty**, LDN Language School, Brazil.

MIDDLE EAST AND NORTH AFRICA

Susan Daniels, Kuwait University, Kuwait; **Mahmoud Mohammadi Khomeini**, Sokhane Ashna Language School, Iran; **Müge Lenbet**, Koç University, Turkey; **Robert Anthony Lowman**, Prince Mohammad bin Fahd University, Saudi Arabia; **Simon Mackay**, Prince Mohammad bin Fahd University, Saudi Arabia.

USA AND CANADA

Frank Abbot, Houston Community College, Houston, TX; **Hossein Aksari**, Bilingual Education Institute and Houston Community College, Houston, TX; **Sudie Allen-Henn**, North Seattle College, Seattle, WA; **Sharon Allie**, Santa Monica Community College, Santa Monica, CA; **Jerry Archer**, Oregon State University, Corvallis, OR; **Nicole Ashton**, Central Piedmont Community College, Charlotte, NC; **Barbara Barrett**, University of Miami, Coral Gables, FL; **Maria Bazan-Myrick**, Houston Community College, Houston, TX; **Rebecca Beal**, Colleges of Marin, Kentfield, CA; **Marlene Beck**, Eastern Michigan University, Ypsilanti, MI; **Michelle Bell**, University of Southern California, Los Angeles, CA; **Linda Bolet**, Houston Community College, Houston, TX; **Jenna Bollinger**, Eastern Michigan University, Ypsilanti, MI; **Monica Boney**, Houston Community College, Houston, TX; **Nanette Bouvier**, Rutgers University – Newark, Newark, NJ; **Nancy Boyer**, Golden West College, Huntington Beach, CA; **Lia Brenneman**, University of Florida English Language Institute, Gainesville, FL; **Colleen Brice**, Grand Valley State University, Allendale, MI; **Kristen Brown**, Massachusetts International Academy, Marlborough, MA; **Philip Brown**, Houston Community

College, Houston, TX; **Dongmei Cao**, San Jose City College, San Jose, CA; **Molly Cheney**, University of Washington, Seattle, WA; **Emily Clark**, The University of Kansas, Lawrence, KS; **Luke Coffelt**, International English Center, Boulder, CO; **William C Cole-French**, MCPHS University, Boston, MA; **Charles Colson**, English Language Institute at Sam Houston State University, Huntsville, TX; **Lucy Condon**, Bilingual Education Institute, Houston, TX; **Janice Crouch**, Internexus Indiana, Indianapolis, IN; **Charlene Dandrow**, Virginia Tech Language and Culture Institute, Blacksburg, VA; **Loretta Davis**, Coastline Community College, Westminster, CA; **Marta Dmytrenko-Ahrabian**, Wayne State University, Detroit, MI; **Bonnie Duhart**, Houston Community College, Houston, TX; **Karen Eichhorn**, International English Center, Boulder, CO; **Tracey Ellis**, Santa Monica Community College, Santa Monica, CA; **Jennifer Evans**, University of Washington, Seattle, WA; **Marla Ewart**, Bilingual Education Institute, Houston, TX; **Rhoda Fagerland**, St. Cloud State University, St. Cloud, MN; **Kelly Montijo Fink**, Kirkwood Community College, Cedar Rapids, IA; **Celeste Flowers**, University of Central Arkansas, Conway, AR; **Kurtis Foster**, Missouri State University, Springfield, MO; **Rachel Garcia**, Bilingual Education Institute, Houston, TX; **Thomas Germain**, University of Colorado Boulder, Boulder, CO; **Claire Gimble**, Virginia International University, Fairfax, VA; **Marilyn Glazer-Weisner**, Middlesex Community College, Lowell, MA; **Amber Goodall**, South Piedmont Community College, Charlotte, NC; **Katya Goussakova**, Seminole State College of Florida, Sanford, FL; **Jane Granado**, Texas State University, San Marcos, TX; **Therea Hampton**, Mercer County Community College, West Windsor Township, NJ; **Jane Hanson**, University of Nebraska – Lincoln, Lincoln, NE; **Lauren Heather**, University of Texas at San Antonio, San Antonio, TX; **Jannette Hermina**, Saginaw Valley State University, Saginaw, MI; **Gail Hernandez**, College of Staten Island, Staten Island, NY; **Beverly Hobbs**, Clark University, Worcester, MA; **Kristin Homuth**, Language Center International, Southfield, MI; **Tim Hooker**, Campbellsville University, Campbellsville, KY; **Raylene Houck**, Idaho State University, Pocatello, ID; **Karen L. Howling**, University of Bridgeport, Bridgeport, CT; **Sharon Jaffe**, Santa Monica Community College, Santa Monica, CA; **Andrea Kahn**, Santa Monica Community College, Santa Monica, CA; **Eden Bradshaw Kaiser**, Massachusetts International Academy, Marlborough, MA; **Mandy Kama**, Georgetown University, Washington, D.C.; **Andrea Kaminski**, University of Michigan – Dearborn, Dearborn, MI; **Phoebe Kang**, Brock University, Ontario; **Eileen Kramer**, Boston University CELOP, Brookline, MA; **Rachel Lachance**, University of New Hampshire, Durham, NH; **Janet Langon**, Glendale Community College, Glendale, CA; **Frances Le Grand**, University of Houston, Houston, TX; **Esther Lee**, California State University, Fullerton, CA; **Helen S. Mays Lefal**, American Learning Institute, Dallas, TX; **Oranit Limmaneeprasert**, American River College, Sacramento, CA; **Dhammika Liyanage**, Bilingual Education Institute, Houston, TX; **Emily Lodmer**, Santa Monica Community College, Santa Monica Community College, CA; **Ari Lopez**, American Learning Institute Dallas, TX; **Nichole Lukas**, University of Dayton, Dayton, OH; **Undarmaa Maamuujav**, California State University, Los Angeles, CA; **Diane Mahin**, University of Miami, Coral Gables, FL; **Melanie Majeski**, Naugatuck Valley Community College, Waterbury, CT; **Judy Marasco**, Santa Monica Community College, Santa Monica, CA; **Murray McMahan**, University of Alberta, Alberta; **Deirdre McMurtry**, University of Nebraska Omaha, Omaha, NE; **Suzanne Meyer**, University of Pittsburgh, Pittsburgh, PA; **Cynthia Miller**, Richland College, Dallas, TX; **Sara Miller**, Houston Community College, Houston, TX; **Gwendolyn Miraglia**, Houston Community College, Houston, TX; **Katie Mitchell**, International English Center, Boulder, CO; **Ruth Williams Moore**, University of Colorado Boulder, Boulder, CO; **Kathy Najafi**, Houston Community College, Houston, TX; **Sandra Navarro**, Glendale Community College, Glendale, CA; **Stephanie Ngom**, Boston University, Boston MA; **Barbara Niemczyk**, University of Bridgeport, Bridgeport, CT; **Melody Nightingale**, Santa Monica Community College, Santa Monica, CA; **Alissa Olgun**, California Language Academy, Los Angeles, CA; **Kimberly Oliver**, Austin Community College, Austin, TX; **Steven Olson**, International English Center, Boulder, CO; **Fernanda Ortiz**, University of Arizona, Tucson, AZ; **Joel Ozretich**, University of Washington, Seattle, WA; **Erin Pak**, Schoolcraft College, Livonia, MI; **Geri Pappas**, University of Michigan – Dearborn, Dearborn, MI; **Eleanor Paterson**, Erie Community College, Buffalo, NY; **Sumeeta Patnaik**, Marshall University, Huntington, WV; **Mary Peacock**, Richland College, Dallas, TX; **Kathryn Porter**, University of Houston, Houston, TX; **Eileen Prince**, Prince Language Associates, Newton Highlands, MA; **Marina Ramirez**, Houston Community College, Houston, TX; **Laura Ramm**, Michigan State University, East Lansing, MI; **Chi Rehg**, University of South Florida, Tampa, FL; **Cyndy Reimer**, Douglas College, New Westminster, British Columbia; **Sydney Rice**, Imperial Valley College, Imperial, CA; **Lynnette Robson**, Mercer University, Macon, GA; **Helen E. Roland**, Miami Dade College, Miami, FL; **Maria Paula Carreira Rolim**, Southeast Missouri State University, Cape Girardeau, MO; **Jill Rolston-Yates**, Texas State University, San Marcos, TX; **David Ross**, Houston Community College, Houston, TX; **Rachel Scheiner**, Seattle Central College, Seattle, WA; **John Schmidt**, Texas Intensive English Program, Austin, TX; **Mariah Schueman**, University of Miami, Coral Gables, FL; **Erika Shadburne**, Austin Community College, Austin, TX; **Mahdi Shamsi**, Houston Community College, Houston, TX; **Osha Sky**, Highline College, Des Moines, WA; **William Slade**, University of Texas, Austin, TX; **Takako Smith**, University of Nebraska – Lincoln, Lincoln, NE; **Barbara Smith-Palinkas**, Hillsborough Community College, Tampa, FL; **Paula Snyder**, University of Missouri, Columbia, MO; **Mary; Evelyn Sorrell**, Bilingual Education Institute, Houston TX; **Kristen Stauffer**, International English Center, Boulder, CO; **Christina Stefanik**, The Language Company, Toledo, OH; **Cory Stewart**, University of Houston, Houston, TX; **Laurie Stusser-McNeill**, Highline College, Des Moines, WA; **Tom Sugawara**, University of Washington, Seattle, WA; **Sara Sulko**, University of Missouri, Columbia, MO; **Mark Sullivan**, University of Colorado Boulder, Boulder, CO; **Olivia Szabo**, Boston University, Boston, MA; **Amber Tallent**, University of Nebraska Omaha, Omaha, NE; **Amy Tate**, Rice University, Houston, USA; **Aya C. Tiacoh**, Bilingual Education Institute, Houston, TX; **Troy Tucker**, Florida SouthWestern State College, Fort Myers, FL; **Anne Tyoan**, Savannah College of Art and Design, Savannah, GA; **Michael Vallee**, International English Center, Boulder, CO; **Andrea Vasquez**, University of Southern Maine, Portland, ME; **Jose Vasquez**, University of Texas Rio Grande Valley, Edinburgh, TX; **Maureen Vendeville**, Savannah Technical College, Savannah, GA; **Melissa Vervinck**, Oakland University, Rochester, MI; **Adriana Villarreal**, Universided Nacional Autonoma de Mexico, San Antonio, TX; **Summer Webb**, International English Center, Boulder, CO; **Mercedes Wilson-Everett**, Houston Community College, Houston, TX; **Lora Yasen**, Tokyo International University of America, Salem, OR; **Dennis Yommer**, Youngstown State University, Youngstown, OH; **Melojeane (Jolene) Zawilinski**, University of Michigan – Flint, Flint, MI.

CREDITS

PHOTOS

Cover KiskaMedia/Getty Images

iii NASA Photo/Alamy Stock Photo, **iv** ©Christopher Anderson/Magnum Photos, **iv** ©Michael Kane, **iv** Zhong Zhi/Getty Images, **iv** CPRESS PHOTO LIMITED / Alamy Stock Photo, **iv** ©Carolyn Drake/Magnum Photos, **vi** AP Images/Solent News/REX Shutterstock, **vi** ©NASA, **vi** The Asahi Shimbun/Getty Images, **vi** ©Carsten Peter/ National Geographic Creative, **vi** JOHN STANMEYER/National Geographic Creative, **viii** scorton / Alamy Stock Photo, **viii** ©Daniel Maher Stained Glass, **001** (c) ©Christopher Anderson/Magnum Photos, **002** (c) Thomas Barwick/Getty Images, **004** (cl) BEVERLY JOUBERT/National Geographic Creative, **005** (br) WILLIAM ALLEN/National Geographic Creative, **006** (t) ANNIE GRIFFITHS/National Geographic Creative, **007** (b) ANNIE GRIFFITHS/National Geographic, **009** (t) View Pictures/ Getty Images, **012** (t) Taylor Weidman/Getty Images, **014** (b) Mel Melcon/Getty Images, **017** (c) TYRONE TURNER/National Geographic Creative, **019** (t) Cengage Learning, Inc., **021** (c) ©Michael Kane, **022-023** (c) Cengage Learning, Inc., **024** (cl) wekeli/Getty Images, **027** (bc) ©Greg Ruffing/Redux, **028** (bc) ©Chris Noble/ Aurora Photos, **031** (bc) DIANE COOK, LEN JENSHEL/National Geographic Creative, **032** (t) Hindustan Times/Getty Images, **034** (bc) MOHAMED ABDIWAHAB/Getty Images, **036** (tc) MICHAEL S. YAMASHITA/National Geographic Creative, **039** (tc) Suzanne Tucker/Shutterstock.com, **041** (c) Zhong Zhi/Getty Images, **042-043** (c) scorton / Alamy Stock Photo, **043** (c) Cengage Learning, Inc., **045** (bc) i love images/Getty Images, **046** (c) tanuha2001/Shutterstock.com, **048** (bc) Juanmonino/ Getty Images, **051** (bc) ©Image Courtesy of The Advertising Archives, **051** (bc) dcwcreations/Shutterstock.com, **052** (t) The Asahi Shimbun/Getty Images, **058** (c) Cengage Learning, Inc., **061** (c) CPRESS PHOTO LIMITED / Alamy Stock Photo, **062-063** (c) ©Marko Korošec/500px, **064** (bc) VCG/Getty Images, **067** (bc) AFP/ Getty Images, **069** (t) JAMES FORTE/National Geographic Creative, **070** (bc) Ilker canikligil/Shutterstock.com, **072** (t) CARSTEN PETER/National Geographic Creative, **075** (br) © 2010 NGM MAPS/National Geographic Image Collection, **076** (t) ©PETER ESSICK/National Geographic Creative, **080** (tr) Cengage Learning, Inc., **081** (c) ©Carolyn Drake/Magnum Photos, **082-083** (c) ©Paulette Tavormina/National Geographic Creative, **084** (cl) ©SCRIPT AND SEAL/National Geographic Creative, **086** (c) Stanisic Vladimir/Shutterstock.com, **086** (c) Africa Studio/Shutterstock.com, **086** (c) Lisovskaya Natalia/Shutterstock.com, **086** (c) Bochkarev Photography/ Shutterstock.com, **089** (t) Addy Ho / EyeEm/Getty Images, **090** (bc) Rich-Joseph Facun/Getty Images, **092** (t) MARTIN BUREAU/Getty Images, **095** (bc) ©CRAIG CUTLER/National Geographic Creative, **096** (bc) Frans Lanting/National Geographic Creative, **098-099** (bc) ©Manuel Canales/National Geographic Creative.

MAPS

75 National Geographic Magazine Maps.

ILLUSTRATIONS/INFOGRAPHICS

19 Adapted from "Mapping Ocean Wealth/Fish Production and Tourism", http://oceanwealth.org/mapping-ocean-wealth-infographics/; **22–23** Adapted from "The Happy Planet Index," http://happyplanetindex.org; **43** Created by 5W, adapted from "The On-Demand Economy" Sachs Insights: http://www.sachsinsights .com/The-On-Demand-Economy; **55** Adapted from "Seven Ingredients for a Successful Content Marketing Strategy" http://theorganicagency.com.au/wp-content /uploads/2015/07/Infographic-7-Ingredients-for-a-Successful-Content-Marketing-Strategy.jpg; **58** Created by 5W, adapted from "Why Your Brain Craves Infographics" http://neomam.com/interactive/13reasons/, "Why do Infographics Make Great Marketing Tools" http://neomam.com/blog/infographics-make-great-marketing -tools/, "Visual Marketing: A Picture's Worth 60,000 Words" http://www.business2community.com/digital-marketing/visual-marketing-pictures-worth-60000-words -01126256#6KSAtH2DhJyGT80M.97; **82–83** Created by 5W, adapted from "Arcadis Sustainable Cities Index", http://downtoearth.danone.com/2015/02/23/50-of-the -worlds-largest-cities-ranked-by-people-planet-profit/, https://www.arcadis.com/en/global/our-perspectives/sustainable-cities-index-2016/.

LISTENING AND TEXT SOURCES

3 Source: Forbes, Statista, Millennial Careers: 2020 Vision; **17** Sources: "Interview With Sylvia Earle" from National Geographic Kids, "Saving the World's Oceans Is This Marine Biologist's Life Pursuit" by Gary Strauss, National Geographic, September 28, 2016; **24** Source: "Funny Business," by David George Gordon: National Geographic World, April 1999; **26–27** Source: "Apes Laugh, Tickle Study Finds" by Brian Handwerk, National Geographic News, June 4, 2009; **35** Source: "City Parks: Space for the Soul," by Jennifer Ackerman: National Geographic Magazine, October 2006; **36–37** Source: "This is Your Brain on Nature" by Florence Williams: National Geographic Magazine, January; **46–47** Sources: "How to Market Your Company Mascot on a Budget" by Ann Smarty, Entrepreneur, March 24, 2017; "How Mascots Work, and How to Pick a Memorable One" by Ira Kalb, Business Insider, January 15, 2012; "America's Most-Loved Spokespersons" by Lacey Rose, Forbes, July 8, 2008; "Mascots most effective in boosting conservation by threatening disapproval" University of Delaware, ScienceDaily, 21 September, 2015; "Mascots: Can a humanlike figure actually harm a company?" Science Daily, July 7, 2015; **51** Sources: https://www.frostedflakes.com/en_US/tony-the-tiger.html; "Tony the Tiger", AdvertisingAge, March 29, 1999; "Tony the Tiger: Mascot of Kellogg's Frosted Flakes", Planet Retro, June 19, 2008; "A Tiger at 60: How Kellogg's Tony Is Changing for a New Age" by E.J. Schultz, AdvertisingAge, August 29, 2011; "Then and Now: The Evolution of Cereal Mascots", Design Shack: https://designshack.net/articles/graphics/then-and-now-the-evolution-of-cereal- mascots/; **63** Sources: "The World's Most Extreme Weather Records" by Michael Kuhne, Accuweather, April 8, 2015; "16 of the Craziest Weather Events We've Seen So Far in 2016" by Chris Dolce, Weather.com, June 26, 2016; "Weirdo Weather: 7 Rare Weather Events" by Live Science Staff, March 2, 2011; "Top 10 Worst Weather Disasters" by DNEWS, December 12, 2012; "Extreme Weather": http://nca2014.globalchange.gov/highlights/report-findings/extreme-weather, "Major weather events cited in the World Meteorological Organisation study": https://s-media-cache-ak0.pinimg.com/originals/c7/6b/e6/c76be6768e398f2df072af29466a8e6d.jpg; **64, 66–67** Sources: "5 Weather Events Happening Right Now That Shouldn't Be" by Jon Erdman, The Weather Channel, January 8, 2016; "Climate change fingerprints seen on 24 weird weather cases, study says" by AP/CBS News, December 15, 2016; "World's Strangest Weather Phenomena" by Jon Erdman, The Weather Channel, April 7, 2014; "Outlook: Extreme—Changing Rains" by Elizabeth Kolbert, National Geographic Magazine, April 2009; **75** Source: "Viking Weather," by Tim Folger: National Geographic

Magazine, June 2010; **76** Source: "Greenland reaps benefits of global warming" by Mathew di Salvo, Independent, March 31, 2013; **87** Sources: "Waste Not, Want Not" by Elizabeth Royte and Brian Finke, National Geographic Magazine, March 2016; "The 5 senses of flavor: How colour and sound can make your dinner taste better" by Ann Hui, The Globe and Mail, March 19, 2013; **96–97** Source: "A Five Step Plan to Feed the World" by Jonathan Foley, George Steinmetz, and Jim Richardson, National Geographic Magazine, May 2014.

INDEX OF EXAM SKILLS AND TASKS

Pathways Listening, Speaking, and Critical Thinking 2nd Edition, is designed to provide practice for standardized exams, such as IELTS and TOEFL. Many activities in this book practice or focus on **key exam skills** needed for test success. Here is an index of activities in Level 1 that are similar to **common questions types** found in these tests.

Listening

Key Exam Skills	IELTS	TOEFL	Page(s) / Exercise(s)
Listening for main ideas	X	X	6 LS, 6 B, 17 E, 27 D, 56 C, 66 C, 87 C, 106 B, 176 B, 187 D
Listening for causes and effects	X	X	146 LS
Listening for key details	X	X	27 E, 37 C, 47 D, 87 C, 107 C, 176 C, 186 LS, 187 D, 187 E
Listening for people's opinions	X	X	167 LS, 167 D
Listening for supporting examples	X	X	47 LS, 47 C, 197 C
Listening for supporting reasons	X	X	87 LS
Making inferences	X	X	7 D, 127 LS, 127 D, 197 CT
Organizing the notes you take	X	X	36 NT, 76 NT, 77 D, 197 NT, 197 C
Taking notes	X	X	79 A
Taking notes on key words and phrases	X	X	7 NT, 7 C
Understanding vocabulary from context	X	X	14 A, 66 LS, 106 LS, 106 A, 107 D, 134 A
Using abbreviations when taking notes	X	X	46 NT, 47 B
Using symbols in your notes	X	X	146 NT

Common Question Types	IELTS	TOEFL	Page(s) / Exercise(s)
Gist-content		X	6 B
Gist-purpose		X	26 B, 156 B
Making inferences		X	7 D, 127 D
Matching	X		67 D
Multiple choice	X	X	37 C, 56 C, 106 B, 116 B, 137 D
Multiple response	X	X	126 B
Note completion	X		107 C, 146 B, 156 C
Sentence completion	X		27 E, 36 B, 137 E
Short answer	X		76 C

KEY

CT	Critical Thinking
EL	Everyday Language
GFS	Grammar for Speaking
LS	Listening Skill
NT	Note-Taking Skill
PRON	Pronunciation
PS	Presentation Skill
SS	Speaking Skill

INDEX OF EXAM SKILLS AND TASKS

Speaking

Key Exam Skills	IELTS	TOEFL	Page(s) / Exercise(s)
Activating prior knowledge	X	X	66 CT
Asking for repetition	X		29 EL
Chunking	X	X	186 PRON, 186 B
Comparing and contrasting	X	X	168 GFS, 171 C, 178 A, 179 E
Expressing agreement or disagreement		X	17 H
Expressing opinions	X	X	7 E, 35 D, 59 D, 73 D, 97 D, 113 F, 129 C, 160 E, 167 F, 185 E
Expressing possibility or probability	X	X	148 GFS, 150 D
Expressing reasons for an opinion	X	X	32 A
Having a strong conclusion	X	X	60 PS
Hedging	X	X	149 SS, 150 E
Linking	X	X	157 PRON, 157 F, 157 H
Making predictions	X		26 CT, 26 A
Pronouncing the ends of words clearly	X	X	56 PRON, 56 A
Reduced forms	X	X	67 PRON, 67 F
Speaking about abstract concepts	X	X	27 F, 77 F, 87 D, 100 D, 133 E, 146 A, 153 G, 165 C, 172 A, 180 E, 190 F, 197 D, 200 C
Speaking about a familiar topic	X	X	40 C
Speaking about habits	X	X	8 GFS, 8 A
Speaking about likes and dislikes	X	X	30 I, 65 D, 78 SS, 78 C, 79 D, 84 C, 171 A
Speaking about pros and cons	X	X	13 E, 132 A, 139 CT, 139 D
Speaking about the future	X		128 PRON, 128 GFS, 129 C, 130 G, 131 D
Speaking about the past	X	X	50 GFS
Speaking about the weather	X	X	73 C
Speaking about where you live	X		111 C, 119 G
Speaking about your life or job	X		20 C, 31 B
Understanding a speaker's purpose	X	X	26 LS
Using correct stress	X	X	16 PRON, 16 A, 16 C, 90 PRON, 90 F, 90 G, 117 PRON, 177 PRON, 177 F
Using descriptive language	X	X	89 GFS
Using time markers	X	X	88 SS, 98 A, 131 D, 131 PS

KEY

CT	Critical Thinking
EL	Everyday Language
GFS	Grammar for Speaking
LS	Listening Skill
NT	Note-Taking Skill
PRON	Pronunciation
PS	Presentation Skill
SS	Speaking Skill

Pathways	CEFR	IELTS Band	TOEFL Score
Level 4	C1	6.5–7.0	81–100
Level 3	B2	5.5–6.0	51–80
Level 2	B1–B2	4.5–5.0	31–50
Level 1	**A2–B1**	**0–4.0**	**0–30**
Foundations	A1–A2		